ADVANCE PRAISE FOR

News Literacy Now

"Finally, a practical approach to combining media literacy with news! This book gives a step-by-step guide to teaching about news through a media literacy lens, providing students and adults alike an accessible and deeper foundation for evaluating the quality and relevance of their media."

—Tessa Jolls, President and CEO of the Center for Media Literacy

"I am grateful to Dr. Eisenstock for writing a book to share not only with students but with friends and family who want to enhance their news literacy skills. Written in an easy to understand and well-designed manner, News Literacy Now: How to '*Read*' the News allows the reader to practice inquiry-based learning as they read. Each chapter comes with key takeaways, guiding questions, and reflection prompts that are appropriate and impactful for all. There is no doubt that understanding how to identify and understand reliable news is of utmost importance to our democracy. We all need to hone our media literacy skills and this book is an excellent guide. I plan to recommend it far and wide."

—Michelle Ciulla Lipkin, Executive Director, National Association for Media Literacy Education

"Eisenstock establishes a framework for judging information that is both intuitive and sophisticated, giving the user a playbook for determining the legitimacy of information. She validates readers' feelings that mis- and disinformation is on the rise, but never makes them feel hopeless. Instead, hers is an empowering message that we can — and should — use the right tools to fight misinformation and help others do the same."

—Barbara Allen, Director of College Programming, The Poynter Institute

News Literacy Now

Bobbie Eisenstock

News Literacy Now

How to "*Read*" the News

PETER LANG
Lausanne • Berlin • Bruxelles • Chennai • New York • Oxford

Library of Congress Cataloging-in-Publication Data

Names: Eisenstock, Bobbie, author.
Title: News literacy now: how to "read" the news / Bobbie Eisenstock.
Description: New York: Peter Lang, [2023] | Includes bibliographical references.
Identifiers: LCCN 2022057735 (print) | LCCN 2022057736 (ebook) | ISBN 9781636670935 (paperback) | ISBN 9781636670942 (hardback) | ISBN 9781636670959 (ebook) | ISBN 9781636670966 (epub)
Subjects: LCSH: Media literacy. | Fake news. | Citizen journalism.
Classification: LCC P96.M4 E55 2023 (print) | LCC P96.M4 (ebook) | DDC 302.23—dc23/eng/20230109
LC record available at https://lccn.loc.gov/2022057735
LC ebook record available at https://lccn.loc.gov/2022057736
DOI 10.3726/b20691

Bibliographic information published by the **Deutsche Nationalbibliothek.**.
The German National Library lists this publication in the German National Bibliography; detailed bibliographic data is available on the Internet at http://dnb.d-nb.de.

Cover design by Peter Lang Group AG

ISBN 9781636670935 (paperback)
ISBN 9781636670942 (hardback)
ISBN 9781636670959 (ebook)
ISBN 9781636670966 (epub)
DOI 10.3726/ b20691

Peter Lang Group AG, Lausanne
Published by Peter Lang Publishing Inc., New York, USA
info@peterlang.com - www.peterlang.com

This publication has been peer reviewed.

To Eyla Shae and the next generation —
may you lead the way to a more caring, equitable, and media literate world

Contents

List of Illustrations

Acknowledgments

The idea for this book was inspired by my students. Their generation is coming of age at a time when it is challenging to know who or what to believe. My hope is that they get into the habit of reading quality journalism and use their news literacy skills to "read" between the lines and become informed and involved citizens who value and protect democracy.

This is not a typical academic book. Thank you Patricia Mulrane Clayton at Peter Lang Group for seeing my vision, and Dani Green, my editor, and Jackie Pavlovic, production manager and quality champion, for helping to realize that vision.

Thank you to all my media literacy colleagues and especially:

Tessa Jolls and the Center for Media Literacy, you have been my backbone for media literacy. Thank you for being a friend and honoring the legacy of Elizabeth Thoman by continuing to make the Center a vital voice of the media literacy movement.

The National Association for Media Literacy Education, I am grateful to be part of a community that does the critical work to educate and advocate for media literacy education, and I am honored to serve on the Board of Directors to help guide its mission.

Jessi Hollis McCarthy at the Freedom Forum, thank you for being my passionate partner in brainstorming new ways to teach students to disrupt disinformation that threatens our democracy.

My appreciation for my colleagues in the Journalism Department at California State University, Northridge runs deep, especially Linda Bowen, who as Chair supported me developing a news literacy course that is the basis for this book.

A special thank you to Kathy Montgomery and Jeff Chester at the Center for Digital Democracy for your support and our impassioned discussions about media, politics, and life over the many years of our friendship.

I am fortunate to have an extraordinary group of friends and family members who are a constant support — thank you Madeline, Phil, Sue, George, Susan, Richard, my walking partner Linda, my sister Susan, and Loretta my lifeline.

There would be no book without the love and support of my family. Jonah and Kiva, I am forever grateful for the joy you bring and for being two of my biggest supporters, as well as my media literacy experiment when you were growing up. Randy, thank you for enriching our family and carrying on the tradition of media-literate parenting with Eyla. And Alan, the LOML, how do I say thank you to a unique human who is always there for me, makes me laugh, keeps me sane, and shares a life in which we mutually create a space to pursue our passions.

Dear Reader

Real news. Fake news. Alternative facts. Post-truths. How do we know what is real or made up? How do we identify reliable and credible news? We are living in the Digital Age of Disinformation when it has become harder and harder to know who and what to believe. How we choose to get our news has never mattered more.

I am a media literacy educator and advocate. I have been teaching for more than three decades and have taught thousands of students, and facilitated workshops for just as many educators, parents, health practitioners, and media professionals. Whether I am teaching about media and diversity or gender or popular culture, my students learn media literacy skills. In my teacher in-service trainings, parent education and professional workshops, media literacy is emphasized as a life skill. I teach how to analyze media messages with a critical eye by asking questions about who created the message and why, the techniques used to construct the message and deconstruct its meaning, and how different people might interpret the message.

Then came the 2016 presidential election. That year the word *post-truth* was chosen by *Oxford English Dictionary* as the word-of-the-year because it spiked in frequency in mainstream media and became associated with the phrase *post-truth politics*. The term "*fake news*" was also popularized and added to the dictionary.

Just when we were steeling ourselves for the 2020 presidential election year, we were hit with Covid-19. By April, news was overwhelmed with misinformation and disinformation about the global pandemic and *Oxford English Dictionary* lexicographers who track and analyze word usage began to release updates of new word entries: *Covid-19, coronavirus, infodemic, self-isolate, self-quarantine, shelter in place, social distancing, superspreader, flatten the curve, PPE, staycation* and more. By June, the Black Lives Matter movement was back in the national headlines after the murders of George Floyd, Breonna Taylor and other Black Americans by police officers that led to protests against law enforcement agencies and a surge of social activism in the United States and around the world. *Black Lives Matter* and its abbreviation *BLM* exploded in usage and were added to the new word list.

With so many events happening worldwide in 2020, *Oxford English Dictionary* decided for the first time in its history that one word could not capture the year and instead chose a list of words that most frequently appeared in text and web-based news, blogs, and other sources. The words were selected from different categories that included Covid-related vocabulary, social movements and social media, new technologies for working and living remotely, the environment, politics, and economics. Among the new word entries in *Oxford Languages 2020: Words of an Unprecedented Year* is one entry that is particularly noteworthy: *media literacy.* The *Oxford English Dictionary* (March 2021) defines media literacy as "proficiency in the evaluation, analysis, and understanding of mass media; *esp.* the ability to analyse critically any story or event presented in the media and to determine its accuracy or credibility."

Although the media literacy movement has been around for decades, the use of the term was relatively rare outside of educational circles. It took "fake news" to bring media literacy out of the academic shadow and into the mainstream. Usage of the term media literacy will undoubtedly become more widespread as misinformation and disinformation continue to gain momentum in the media ecosystem increasing the need for skills to separate fact from fiction. There are plenty of indications that conspiracy theorists, hate groups, certain news personalities and news outlets, social media users, even some elected officials, are attempting to create an alternative reality. Consider the false narrative that emerged following the 2020 election claiming that Trump was robbed of his second term as president through election fraud.

The "Big Lie," as it is called, stands out for its gross intentional misrepresentation of the facts and polarizing effect on the country. This manipulation of the election facts to delegitimize the new Administration incited the January

6th insurrection on the U.S. Capitol in which thousands stormed the building during a violent mob attack against the U.S. Congress. The attack terrorized members of Congress, their staffs, and the press, and resulted in multiple deaths, physical harm to over 140 law enforcement officials, and a heightened threat environment across the country. Two days later Twitter permanently suspended Trump's account "due to the risk of further incitement of violence" (Twitter, 2021). Still, as hundreds of rioters were arrested for their role in the insurrection and charged with assaulting police officers, illegal entry into government buildings and desecrating government property, some news pundits, elected officials, including former President Trump, attempted to rebrand the deadly insurrection as a "love fest" or characterize it as "a normal tourist visit." The Republican National Committee Chair attempted to justify the deadly riot as "legitimate public discourse." While this blatant mischaracterization was refuted by Senate Republican Minority Leader Mitch McConnell who called it a "violent insurrection," others in the party did not side with him.

More than a year later, the ideologically motivated "Big Lie" continues to be promoted by Trump, many Republican politicians and their supporters, as well as conservative TV news personalities and talk show hosts, and Trump's Twitter account has been reinstated by new ownership. Polls show a majority of Republicans falsely believe there was election fraud and are not swayed by incriminating evidence presented by the House Select Committee investigation or the rare charge of seditious conspiracy brought by the Justice Department against several insurrectionists for their role in the attack. The lie also has had a ripple effect on future elections. "Big Lie" believers are putting the future of fair elections in jeopardy by doxxing, harassing and threatening election workers for doing their job, and candidates who promote the lie are running for office where they would exert influence over the way ballots are cast, counted and certified.

Clearly, teaching media literacy concepts is not enough to understand what is happening with news messaging, especially during times of crisis when new information is rapidly developing. What is missing is knowledge about journalism practices and standards and skills to assess the news source, check the facts, and empower civic responsibility and engagement. With my background in journalism and media literacy, I developed a News Literacy course for the journalism program where I teach that connects media literacy and news literacy concepts with civic engagement.

This book is about the essential news media literacy skills every person should know to help navigate the complex news media ecosystem. I truly hope that this approach helps you become a more news literate person… and that you pass it along!

Bobbie Eisenstock, Ph.D.

References

Oxford English Dictionary. (2020). *Oxford languages 2020: Words of an unprecedented year.* https://languages.oup.com/word-of-the-year/2020/

Oxford English Dictionary. (2021). *New words list March 2021.* https://public.oed.com/updates/new-words-list-march-2021/

Twitter. (2021, January 8). Permanent suspension of @realDonaldTrump. https://blog.twitter.com/en_us/topics/company/2020/suspension

How to Read This Book

If you are familiar with media literacy, this book is for you. And if you are not familiar with media literacy, this book is for you. Here is why.

News Literacy Now: How to "Read" the News is about a new approach to building critical thinking skills for news literacy. Based on the intersection of media literacy, news literacy and web literacy skills, this hybrid strategy adapts the media literacy framework developed by the Center for Media Literacy (CML) to analyze the nature of news and the practice of journalism, apply lateral reading and other fact-checking strategies to verify information, and empower responsible participation in democracy in the ever-changing digital media ecosystem.

The CML framework uses five core concepts and corresponding key questions to analyze media messages. The five concepts focus on authorship, format, content, purpose, and audience. Each core concept and key question is adapted for news messaging and additional questions about the news process guide the analysis. For example, the media literacy core concept about authorship states: "All media messages are constructed." Adapting it for news, it is reworded: "All news stories are constructed." Key questions specifically probe the news-gathering process to identify who wrote the news story, explain how news reporters differ from investigative, feature, and opinion writers, and distinguish between professional journalists and others who generate news such as citizen journalists, bloggers, pundits, news-writing bots and chatbots. (All references to CML's Core Concepts, Key Questions and Keywords are used with permission of the Center for Media Literacy, www.Medialit.org.)

Whether you consider yourself media literate and want to apply the core concepts specifically to news, or a newbie to media and news literacy who needs a primer in how to "read" the news, this book will help you think like a journalist and apply standards to judge the credibility and reliability of information and the trustworthiness of news sources. It is written in an inquiry-based style from the news consumers' perspective, asking and answering questions to think critically about our personal news experiences and provide a context to understand the news process and journalism practices.

The book begins by posing the dilemma we find ourselves facing as news consumers and informed citizens: challenged by a news credibility crisis, how do we know what is real or fake? How do we find trustworthy news sources in a media environment that intermixes real news, misinformation, and disinformation? The first chapter raises questions that we all should consider about our personal news habits and how our biases can trap us in filter bubbles and encircle us in echo chambers.

The second chapter explains why news literacy matters, that most people are not very news literate, and what we need to know to become news literate. This chapter reviews relevant news literacy research and pedagogy to provide a context for understanding how educators are rethinking news literacy strategies. It also explains CML's evidence-based method of inquiry used in developing the news media literacy framework that organizes the structure of this book.

The next five chapters apply CML's five core concepts to news and the practice of journalism one concept at a time. Each chapter focuses on a different core concept and provides guiding questions to deconstruct news stories, the news-gathering process, and the role news audience's play in the changing news media ecosystem. The chapters close with a section entitled "Ask the Right Questions" that illustrates the media-news literacy connection, summarizes key takeaways, and poses questions to probe deeper into the concept explained in the chapter.

The last chapter of the book digs deeper into strategies to help navigate the news media ecosystem in a post-truth culture and become the most news literate consumers we can be. It explains how to search like a fact-checker using lateral reading and other techniques to investigate the source, evaluate the evidence and verify the claims, and suggests ways to talk to someone who believes disinformation. Following this chapter, there are some final words about the need for news media literacy, and a few resources to help identify different types of misinformation and disinformation and learn more about media and news literacy programs, research, and organizations to continue to develop your skills.

A word about definitions. The term misinformation typically is used as a catchall to refer to both misinformation and disinformation. In this book, I differentiate between different types of information based on whether the intent is to inform, mislead or harm. *Misinformation* refers to unintentional reporting errors that will be corrected by a news outlet, whereas *disinformation* is false information that is intentionally created to mislead and cause harm. When people share information that they do not realize is false and misleading, it is *misinformation* and not disinformation because their intention is to inform and not to mislead or harm. *Malinformation*, another type of intentionally harmful information, refers to publicly disclosing private information to deliberately inflict harm on a person, group, company or institution. Also note that at times the terms misinformation, disinformation and malinformation are shortened to mis/dis/malinformation or simply mis/disinformation.

1 You and News

Are you overwhelmed by news? You're not alone.

News finds us wherever we are, even if we're not looking for it. Every day media floods our digital devices with what seems like an endless stream of messages and images. It is a case of information overload or TMI — *too much information*, too much data, too much news. And not all of it is credible. Some of the information is inaccurate or created to intentionally spread falsehoods, rumors or gossip. We are challenged to sift through it all to find what is important and figure out whom to believe.

At a time of crisis like a terrorist attack, natural disaster or global pandemic, when it is vital that the public gets accurate and reliable messaging, this excessive amount of information produces what experts call an *infodemic* — the daily spread of new information, misinformation, and disinformation in the form of rumors, hoaxes and conspiracy theories that can create confusion and build distrust in the media delivering the message. In the pandemic example, the infodemic muddles the messaging about the protocols the public should follow to minimize health risks and causes uncertainty that can hinder an effective public health response to the crisis (World Health Organization, n.d.).

No matter what the infodemic is about, social media amplifies false news by spreading it faster and farther than fact-based news. This is because rumors and conspiracy theories are more likely to be retweeted and shared on social media than factual news making it easier to stumble on them. Consider the conspiracy theories about Covid-19 that have spread on social media. Did you know that 5G mobile phone technology can cause Covid? Or that ivermectin used to treat parasites in horses can prevent the virus in humans? Or that the Covid-19 vaccine causes your body to magnetize? If we get news from social media, we just might believe these false and harmful claims. If we were news literate, we would have skills to "read" the news, to think critically when we navigate the information universe and find credible and trustworthy sources to debunk false claims.

How Do We Get News Literate?

News media literacy is about questioning and challenging what we see, hear and read. That means being open-minded and searching alternative sources to draw our own conclusions. For many of us, that may not come easy because we are not in the habit of doing this. Instead of taking time to critically read the news, we turn to trusted news outlets or social media for news and take what they say at face value, no questions asked, because it reinforces our beliefs and confirms our biases. We end up trapped in filter bubbles that circumscribe our personal online experiences and confined to echo chambers where news affirms our views and confirmation bias affects how we experience the world.

Becoming news literate takes practice. It takes practice to develop the critical thinking skills to determine if a news story is factual or fraudulent, a tweet or quote is credible or hearsay, a meme or GIF is simply humorous or propaganda, or whether or not to believe a particular politician, pundit, talk show host, celebrity or social media influencer when they comment about the news. To jump-start our news literacy skills, it is helpful to examine where we get our news and how our news preferences influence our view of the world.

Five Questions to Ask Ourselves About News

Most people now are tech savvy, at least to some extent. We know how to use computers and smartphones, download an app, and post comments on social media. If we are tech savvy, does that mean we are media literate? Not at all. We may be tech savvy, but not media literate, and probably not news literate. To start developing news literacy skills, consider these five questions:

- ✓ Where do I get my news?
- ✓ How do I know if I am in a filter bubble?
- ✓ How do I know if my news choices are echo chambers?
- ✓ Does confirmation bias limit my worldview?
- ✓ How can I burst my filter bubble, escape my echo chamber, and keep my confirmation bias in check?

Where do we get our news?

Most of us get our news when, where, and how we want it on our mobile devices. That was not the case just a few years ago.

News habits have changed along with news formats and delivery options. No longer is the morning newspaper that arrives at the front door the go-to source for news. Instead we check our smartphones or tablets for the digital version of the newspaper or skim the stories on a news aggregator that launches when we check our email or browse online. Or we skip the newspaper altogether and jump to Twitter, Facebook, Instagram, TikTok or other favorite social media network, news app or podcast, or curate a newsfeed on social media with the type of stories we like. Most of us go online for news because we want it fast, visually stimulating, not too long, and tailored to our interests with 24/7 access.

Where we choose to get our news is more important than we might think. Not only does news raise awareness about what is happening in our community and the world, it cultivates attitudes and opinions and shapes perceptions that reflect the way the news outlet covers the story. If the news we choose has a hyperpartisan point of view or misrepresents certain facts or spreads disinformation, then that perspective influences our views and, in turn, reinforces our biases.

And, thanks to social media, without any training, we've graduated from being media consumers to content creators who contribute to the news cycle. We are *prosumers* — content producers and content consumers who actively participate in the media environment. When we tweet, post, blog, upload a video or photo, we essentially produce content and become our own publishers. Plus, with every "like" or post we share, we promote other publishers, many of whom are not fact-based journalists from news organizations.

How do we know if what we share is accurate and truthful? Do you check if the information is credible and the site is trustworthy? Can you distinguish between opinion, facts and falsehoods? Can you identify a hoax, cynical clickbait, conspiracy theory or other type of disinformation? Or do you not pay attention to where the information originates and allow your own bias to inform you?

The bottom line is, not all news is created equal. To see the big picture, be aware of the web we weave that encircles us in filter bubbles and echo chambers that confirm our biases. We need to be open-minded and get our news from multiple sources with different perspectives, and we need to check the facts. Next time before you share, think critically about what you share.

How do we know if we are in a filter bubble?

What exactly is a filter bubble? A *filter bubble* describes the circumstance in which we find ourselves when we come across only ideas, people, facts and information that are consistent with our viewpoint and reflect our interests (Pariser, 2011). If online content we encounter reinforces only our views and not others, then we are in a filter bubble. If ad after ad pops up on our screen for products we have researched, purchased or simply browsed, that is a filter bubble too. Why does this happen? The answer is *algorithms*.

Filter bubbles result from algorithms that affect what we see online. Think of an algorithm as a set of rules that computes a unique personalized online experience. Google, Facebook, Twitter, Instagram and other social media companies use algorithms to customize services for individual users based on their search history, click behavior, location, age, gender, interests and other data. This sounds like a great idea to navigate the Internet more easily. Not necessarily.

Personalized content selection can be good and bad. It is good because it can create a more enjoyable and streamlined online experience, even when it comes to the news. If we curate quality journalism, then we can readily access this news. It is bad because algorithms can take us down a digital rabbit hole that prevents us from being exposed to new ideas and points of view, or worse, subjects us to unseemly or toxic content that we were not looking for in the first place such as conspiracy theories and other types of disinformation. The more we click, the farther we can fall into the algorithmic-driven rabbit hole. That's because algorithms dictate and delimit which ideas and information we encounter and can enclose us in a filter bubble constructed from our personal data and preexisting opinions and beliefs.

If a set of algorithms creates a *bot* (short for "robot") — a computer program that performs automated tasks and can simulate human activity — it can create content on social media and generate messages to interact with people. Bots can act like followers and infiltrate a group to advocate ideas or create fake accounts to gain followers who propagate disinformation. More sophisticated chatbots can simulate conversations and may promote false and misleading ideas in credible and compelling ways. The person we think we are retweeting or exchanging comments and sharing them on social media may actually be a bot.

How do we know if our news choices are echo chambers?

If we get our news from a source that reinforces our views and feeds our opinions, that just might be an echo chamber. An *echo chamber* refers to a closed system such as a news outlet, newsfeed, talk show, podcast or social media platform that amplifies and reinforces certain viewpoints by repeating them over and over and discredits alternative points of view or excludes them from being communicated. Echo chambers are usually driven by political ideologies and close us off to new or conflicting views, oppositional research, and fact-based discussions that do not support the hardline position of the media outlet or news source. That means that critical issues — such as healthcare, climate crisis, gun safety, immigration, racial inequality, wealth gap, LGBTQ+ and women's rights — may not be given the opportunity to be heard from all sides.

Whether politically right-leaning or left-leaning or somewhere in the middle, echo chambers can contribute to bolstering hyper-partisan politics and deepening political polarization, especially during election years. When politics, algorithms and social media bots interact, it can lead to manipulating public opinion, stifling political speech, amplifying hate speech, and spreading disinformation. Researchers who study this phenomenon call it *computational propaganda* — a circumstance in which algorithms and social media bots, often along with trolls, are programmed to purposefully spread misleading information in order to propagate attacks on the political opposition and drive divisions within society (Woolley & Howard, 2017). Computational propaganda messages that reinforce people's existing opinions and beliefs make them more likely to believe the information and share it online, regardless of its accuracy or reliability.

Have you or someone you know fallen down a "foxhole"?

Echo chambers are like foxholes in which we take shelter from enemy fire, except when it comes to news, we retreat into the echo chamber that provides comfort for our beliefs, usually political beliefs. An example of the echo chamber effect is the influence of Fox News on its viewers. A survey (Navigator Research, 2019) of Fox News viewers found a vastly different alternative political reality promoted by Fox News skewed public opinion about social issues such as climate change, the border wall, and Russian interference in the 2016 election. For example, the survey found that Republicans who did not watch Fox News were more than twice as likely as "Foxhole" Republicans to believe that climate change is mostly caused by humans.

Political scientists call this *partisan coverage filtering bias* — that is, when news outlets selectively choose topics and report only information that is favorable to their partisan or ideological viewpoint and omit what is unfavorable. Slanted coverage can affect viewers' beliefs and attitudes because they get biased information and not the whole story. What would happen if viewers switched news outlets? To find this out researchers paid over 700 regular Fox News viewers, who were highly politically-engaged Republicans, to watch CNN for a month. Here is what they found.

Fox News viewers became more skeptical of biased coverage and shifted their perception of certain social and political issues, such as outbreaks of social justice protests, the seriousness of Covid-19, support for mail-in ballots, mistakes Trump made during his presidency, and evaluation of key Republican politicians. A follow-up survey two months later found that, for the most part, Fox News viewers returned to their old media diet along with their partisan worldview. The researchers caution that intentionally filtering information about partisan issues that impact elections poses a serious challenge to democratic accountability because voters may lack the facts they need to hold politicians accountable (Broockman & Kalla, 2022).

Such a concerning partisan pattern is evident in Fox News' coverage of the January 6, 2021 attack on the U.S. Capitol and the events that followed. Fox News framed the attack and its impact as less serious than it was and the House Select Committee's investigation into the attacks as a partisan probe. Over the next 17 months, Fox News was far less likely than their competitors CNN and MSNBC to mention the attack, the House Select Committee's investigation into the attack, or the extremist groups who stormed the Capitol and the seditious conspiracy charges that some of their members were facing (Bump, 2022). On June 9, 2022, when the House Select Committee televised its first hearing live during primetime, Fox News was the only major news outlet that did not interrupt its regular programming to carry the hearings. In a press release, they said that "Fox News Channel's primetime programs will cover the hearings as news warrants" and instead live coverage would be aired on their less viewed platforms (Fox News Media, 2022). As the hearing was in progress, the most popular Fox News opinion hosts downplayed the enormity of the insurrection, calling out the first hearing as "propaganda" and a "sham" while accusing other networks who broadcast it as "colluding with Democrats."

Don't let the term "foxhole" fool you because it sounds like Fox News. News foxholes are not limited to right-learning media. Any ideologically-driven echo chamber can be a foxhole. In fact, a Pew Research study of the 2020 presidential election found quite striking results. Not only did the majority of Republicans and Democrats consistently stay in their respective left-leaning or right-leaning partisan echo chambers for election information, but Republicans overwhelmingly chose Fox News as their number one trusted source for political news. Democrats, on the other hand, trusted a number of sources, including CNN, MSNBC, BBC, PBS, NPR, and the major mainstream newspapers (Pew Research Center, 2020). Pew Research Center's American News Pathways Project (2021), which examines where Americans get their information on a variety of topics, found that we are essentially living in different information environments and experience divergent realities that confirm our biases but are politically polarizing.

Does confirmation bias limit our worldview?

The short answer is, yes. It is human nature to seek out people, ideas and information that confirm our biases and beliefs and to avoid what does not support them. Check your search history or newsfeed and you will probably notice a pattern that confirms this tendency. The consequences can limit our worldview and inadvertently trap us in a filter bubble and constrain us to an echo chamber. We may not even be aware that we make judgments and evaluate information based on our biases because, for the most part, it happens unconsciously.

Confirmation bias is when we look for, interpret and trust only information that confirms our existing beliefs or attitudes, and reject information that does not support them. We are drawn to echo chambers because they reinforce our attitudes, beliefs and biases. When we enter an echo chamber, we leave logic and objective reasoning at the door and confirmation bias takes over. We trust the information in the echo chamber, accept it unquestioningly, and interpret it as supporting our views. The views are those of our "in-group" and we do not want or need to look further for information that might challenge these views. If the information relates to an emotionally-charged issue about which we have deeply-held convictions, then our biases are strengthened all the more, even in the face of contradictory fact-checked evidence. In fact, we tend to be skeptical of information that contradicts our preexisting belief or point of view. An attack on an issue or our candidate can feel like an attack on ourselves and lead us to retreat to our echo chamber where the information nurtures our biases.

Confirmation bias is a type of unconscious bias that influences the choices we make and how we experience the world. There are many other unconscious biases that get in the way of accepting information without questioning its accuracy and not considering alternative perspectives. Consider a few:

- *anchoring bias:* we put too much trust in the first piece of information we come across and do not take into account other perspectives
- *bandwagon bias:* we adopt certain opinions, beliefs or behaviors because they're popular
- *blind spot bias:* we recognize bias in other people but not in ourselves
- *in-group bias:* we favor those whom we perceive to be like us because they belong to the same group based on ideology, age, race, gender, geography or another similar trait
- *negativity bias:* we focus so much on negative events that we overlook positive or neutral events
- *outcome bias:* we make a decision based solely on the outcome of previous events rather than factors related to the process that led to the decision and could change future outcomes

All types of unconscious bias can make us vulnerable to disinformation. That's because we are susceptible to misleading and false information — hoaxes, rumors, conspiracy theories, and other untrue and inaccurate reporting by media that we trust and depend on for news. We may not discern that it is based on flawed or deceptive data or fallacious arguments that can be disproven with reasoning. Then when we spread incorrect or fraudulent news through likes and shares, it perpetuates the disinformation. Even if the information is disproven, it is nearly impossible to correct because the message has already been widely disseminated and resounds, over and over again, in the echo chamber and beyond. To compound this situation, few will believe the corrected version because their judgment is flawed by their bias.

How do we know if confirmation bias is affecting our views?

While most of us do not consider ourselves biased, we are all affected by unconscious bias, some of us more than others. How much we are influenced depends on the extent to which we recognize our own biases, how open we are to alternative views, and the quality of the sources we use to fact-check information. Even if we recognize our bias, seek out multiple opposing sources and fact-check the information, confirmation bias can cause us to selectively hear what we want to hear, believe what we want to believe and lead us to be wrong because of our belief.

Think about a time when you tried to change someone's mind or simply get the person to consider another point of view. Were you successful or did unconscious bias play a role in their logic? If you presented contradictory facts or compelling opposing evidence and they still could not even consider these alternative views, then some type of cognitive bias is unconsciously flawing their judgment. Perhaps blind spot bias is obstructing their view, or anchoring bias has a grip on their understanding of the issue, or confirmation bias is preventing them from accepting a perspective that challenges their beliefs.

The next time someone voices an opposing viewpoint or tries to convince us that our reasoning might be flawed, consider that we may not entirely understand what we think we understand or that we may not have heard what the other person actually intended us to hear. If we can recognize that our biases may sometimes flaw our judgment, then we might be more open to other views and do some research into the facts before we draw conclusions.

How can we burst our filter bubble, escape our echo chamber, and keep our confirmation bias in check?

The short answer is *get news literate*. There is no formula or top 10 tip list to check off. We need to learn to ask the right questions and apply strategies to dig deeper into what we are reading, watching, and hearing about the news. That takes learning to think like a journalist and search like a fact-checker. By the end of this book, you will have the knowledge and skills to burst your filter bubble, escape your echo chamber, and keep your confirmation bias in check.

Read the Research

It is always of value to understand how we got to a certain point and how we get to the next one. Research can help us do that. Many of us avoid doing or even reading research because we think it is not important or too difficult to comprehend. The truth is research is invaluable in our daily lives. It expands our knowledge and informs our actions. It helps us problem solve and develop new skills. Research helps us learn how to "read" the news. The next chapter reviews relevant research studies to provide a context for understanding what news literacy is, why news literacy matters, and what it means to be a news media literate person.

References

Broockman, D., & Kalla, J. (2022, September 1). The manifold effects of partisan media on viewers' beliefs and attitudes: A field experiment with Fox News' viewers. https://osf.io/jrw26/

Bump, P. (2022, June 7). Of course Fox News isn't airing the Jan 6th committee hearing. *The Washington Post.* https://www.washingtonpost.com/politics/2022/06/07/course-fox-news-isnt-airing-jan-6-committee-hearings/

Fox News Media. (2022, June 6). *Fox News Media to present live coverage of the primetime January 6th hearing on Thursday, June 9 across all platforms* [Press release]. https://press.foxnews.com/2022/06/fox-news-media-to-present-live-coverage-of-the-primetime-january-6th-hearing-on-thursday-june-9th-across-all-platforms

Navigator Research. (2019, March 21). *Stepping inside the foxhole: The media echo-chamber of Fox News.* Navigator Research in collaboration with Global Strategy Group and GBA Strategies. https://navigatorresearch.org/stepping-inside-the-fox-hole/

Pariser, E. (2011). *Filter bubbles: How the new personalized web is changing what we read and how we think.* Penguin Books.

Pew Research Center. (2021, February). *How Americans navigated the news in 2020: A tumultuous year in review.* https://www.journalism.org/2021/02/22/how-americans-navigated-the-news-in-2020-a-tumultuous-year-in-review/

Pew Research Center. (2020, January). *U.S. media polarization and the 2020 election: A nation divided.* https://www.journalism.org/2020/01/24/u-s-media-polarization-and-the-2020-election-a-nation-divided/

Woolley, S., & Howard. P. (2017). *Computational propaganda worldwide: Executive summary.* Working Paper No. 2017.11. Oxford, U.K.: Project on Computational Propaganda. https://demtech.oii.ox.ac.uk/wp-content/uploads/sites/89/2017/06/Casestudies-ExecutiveSummary.pdf

World Health Organization. (n.d.). Infodemic. https://www.who.int/health-topics/infodemic#tab=tab_1

2 Why News Literacy Matters

Why does news literacy matter? Some say that news literacy matters because we live in the Digital Age of Disinformation. That's true. But the truth is that news literacy has always mattered. The public has always needed to be able to determine the veracity of news to be informed and responsibly participate in democracy.

Think about it. Just as the role of the press is to serve as a watchdog for wrongdoing on the public's behalf in a democracy, the public, in turn, has a responsibility to act as a watchdog of truth for themselves wherever they get their news. The public's watchdog role requires a healthy skepticism and not cynicism about the news. Instead of being distrustful of media, we need to become more discerning news consumers. News literacy can help develop actionable skepticism, skills to question and challenge what we see, hear and read, and an understanding of the unique and vital role of journalism in a democracy. Perhaps, in the Digital Age of Disinformation, news literacy has never mattered more because of the glut of false and misleading news and information that has been unleashed into the digital media ecosystem and impacts our democratic values.

Why Do We Need News Literacy Now?

There really has never been a more important time to be news literate. Why now? The simple answer is the Internet. More specifically, the Internet-enabled participatory culture. The digital communications revolution has changed the way we communicate and empowered everyone with access to technology to consume and produce content in the online environment. Anyone can publish on the Internet without oversight. Facts, alternative facts, opinion, satire, and outright lies exist side-by-side on web pages and social media platforms. The Internet, especially social media, has facilitated the spread of misinformation and disinformation creating fodder for a post-truth culture in which emotional appeals and personal beliefs are as or more influential in shaping public opinion than shared objective standards for truth.

Social media is not only a spreader of false information, it is where many of us get our news. According to reports from the Pew Research Center (2021) that track Americans' media habits, more people are turning to social media as a main source of news, but they are not necessarily getting news based on the facts. The study found that people who rely on social media for news tend to know less about politics and current events and more about conspiracy theories and other types of unverified stories that spread online. And, not surprising, people who get their news mainly from social media are more likely to believe rumors and conspiracy theories than people who do not depend on social media for news (Pew Research Center, 2020a). There is also evidence that people who believe conspiracy theories tend to know little about how news is produced, but the more they understand the news-gathering process and commercial context within which news is produced and its effects, the less likely they are to believe conspiracy theories, even when the conspiracy theory supports their political ideology (Craft et al., 2017).

The erosion of our news media ecosystem is real. It is challenging to separate fact from fiction when falsehoods intended to misrepresent the facts and mislead the public are mixed with real news. If what we think is reliable news is not actually reliable, then how do we identify trustworthy sources? Even the most tech savvy of us find that hard to know. Faced with a news credibility crisis, we need critical thinking skills to determine for ourselves what information is reliable or deceptive, even intentionally manipulated to obscure the truth, and know why that matters. We need to develop the ability to identify quality journalism, authenticate news reports, search alternative sources to debunk false claims and draw our own conclusions. News literacy skills are essential life skills that help us think critically to make informed decisions, solve problems, communicate effectively, and wisely navigate the ever-evolving media ecosystem to responsibly participate in a digital democracy.

How News Literate Are We? What the Research Says

The short answer is, not very. What we know from the research is that, regardless of our age or education, we may be news aware but not news literate.

The most telling evidence is from researchers at the Stanford History Education Group (SHEG) focused on developing an informed citizenry who have the skills to judge the reliability and credibility of news and information. In 2016, SHEG researchers (Wineburg et al., 2016) used the word "bleak" to sum up their survey of thousands of middle, high school and college students' digital civic online reasoning skills. The majority of students could not distinguish advertising from news articles, discern fake from factual news, identify the source of a news story or detect political bias in their social media — Facebook pages, Twitter feeds, forum comments, and blog posts.

In 2019, SHEG researchers (Breakstone et al., 2019, 2021b) followed up with a national survey of more than 3,000 high school students and found little improvement in their ability to identify trustworthy sources. When given tasks to evaluate online information, most students assessed websites at face value and did not evaluate the source or fact-check the evidence. Some did better than others — students who attended urban schools outperformed those in suburban and rural schools, and Black/African American students received the lowest scores of all students.

Considering the survey results of the high school students, it is not surprising that SHEG researchers (Wineburg et al., 2020) found that college students lack the essential critical thinking skills to wisely navigate the emerging digital media ecosystem. Sophomores, juniors and seniors were easily duped by a satirical news story believing it to be a credible news report and a website claiming to be nonpartisan when in fact it was partisan. Why is this? The researchers concluded that one of the main reasons is that the strategies taught at colleges and universities are outdated and more applicable to print than online, making students susceptible to misinformation, disinformation, scammers, bad actors and hate mongers. They recommend web savvy strategies practiced by professional fact-checkers such as reading laterally across multiple webpages to evaluate the credibility of the source, responsible use of Wikipedia to initially fact-check, and basic Google keyword and reverse image search skills to check the reliability of the information.

Clearly, the evaluation tools students use have not kept pace with advances in technology and the complexity of the ever-evolving digital media ecosystem. Young people's lack of skills poses a critical concern about their ability to become informed citizens who can responsibly participate in civic life that relies on their ability to access reliable and trustworthy information. This concern led SHEG to develop an evidence-based Civic Online Reasoning (COR) curriculum driven by three key questions fact-checkers ask to evaluate and verify sources: (1) Who's behind the information? (2) What's the evidence? (3) What do other sources say? The curriculum explains and demonstrates strategies to investigate the source of the information, evaluate the relevance and reliability of different forms of evidence, and establish the accuracy of the information by cross-checking and corroborating it with other sources. The goal is to help students learn to make quick but accurate judgments about the value and quality of the different types of information they interact with on their smartphones, tablets, and computers from websites, to tweets and posts on Facebook and Instagram, to videos on YouTube and TikTok (Stanford History Education Group, n.d.).

How effective is SHEG's approach to evaluating digital content? SHEG researchers have been testing the curriculum in a variety of settings and subject areas. And the news is good. Their research indicates that this approach is proving to be effective for teaching students to identify credible and trustworthy online sources. For example, in one study of an entire high school district, half the students enrolled in a required government course completed six lessons in lateral reading techniques and the other half did not. The students who completed the lessons, which were taught by their teachers who attended a one-day professional development workshop to learn the COR techniques, significantly improved their ability to judge the credibility of digital content (Wineburg et al., 2022). In another study, after completing eight lessons to evaluate online sources, high school history students significantly improved their ability to research the source of a website, evaluate evidence for complex and often contentious social and political claims, and find reliable sources (McGrew, 2020). An exploratory study of college students enrolled in a synchronous critical thinking and writing course found that their ability to accurately assess the credibility of digital information improved after two modules that focused on a few professional fact-checking practices (McGrew et al., 2019). College students enrolled in an online asynchronous nutrition course also significantly improved their lateral reading skills after completing four modules (Breakstone et al., 2021a).

While the findings suggest that this approach is an effective way to teach fact-checking strategies across disciplines in different educational settings, the researchers caution that students need support and practice applying these methods in their everyday lives. In a teaching and learning environment that has been driven online by a pandemic, coupled with a digital information ecosystem that increasingly intermixes facts, opinions and falsehoods, these skills are vital to fostering the next generation of informed citizens.

Search like a fact-checker

Teaching lateral reading strategies to search like a professional fact-checker is gaining momentum as a skill set to build citizenship and debunk false and misleading information on social media. An example is the Digital Polarization Initiative (DPI), a national effort by the American Democracy Project to advance civic literacy, which focuses on lateral reading to improve college students' ability to evaluate online information. College students who were taught lateral reading skills in a general education civics course were able to correctly evaluate the trustworthiness of a source (Brodsky et al., 2021). Another example is the CTRL-F program, named for the keyboard shortcut for "find," developed to increase awareness of disinformation and improve online verification skills of Canadian middle and high school students. Teachers were trained to teach their students lateral reading skills and found that the students dramatically improved their ability to reject false claims and identify credible sources and retained these skills six weeks later in a follow-up survey (Pavlounis et al., 2021).

There are signs that professional fact-checking strategies are finding their way into academia, community programs, and journalism initiatives. Consider three examples. Aside from news literacy courses or modules that teach fact-checking to middle, high school and college students, LibGuides developed by librarians to curate knowledge and share information in a specific subject area are starting to include lateral reading skills. An example is the toolkit created by Rowan University librarians to help students develop lateral reading to determine who and what to trust in the online information environment. A preliminary study of students who completed a tutorial based on the toolkit indicated that lateral reading notably improved their evaluation strategies (Baer & Kipnis, 2020). The community program Truth Check uses lateral reading in its self-guided media literacy training toolkit to spot false claims, hoaxes and outright lies about Covid-19 and vaccinations on social media (Truth Check, n.d.). The program is led by the Center for Black Health & Equity, and funded by the Centers for Disease

Control Foundation, to reach Black audiences who experience disproportionately higher rates of Covid-19 infection and death. The goal is to build awareness about mis/disinformation in newsfeeds and provide skills to make informed health decisions.

A groundbreaking approach to teaching professional fact-checking strategies is the Poynter Institute's MediaWise initiative that combines SHEG's curriculum with journalism ethics to teach digital media literacy skills to people of all ages. A central component of the MediaWise program is its Campus Correspondents and Teen Fact-Checking Network, a virtual newsroom in which high school and college students teach their peers to be critical news consumers and make informed decisions based on facts. The students use social media storytelling to visually show step-by-step how to search like a fact-checker to detect and debunk mis/disinformation. The same skills are taught to older adults as part of the MediaWise for Seniors self-directed interactive modules. This is noteworthy because older adults are especially susceptible to false and misleading news online and more likely to share it on Facebook than younger people (Guess et al., 2019). Researchers studied this program during the 2020 presidential election and found it to be effective to help seniors separate fact from fiction — older adults who were taught professional fact-checking skills were more likely to identify fraudulent news and information online than their counterparts who did not take the training (Moore & Hancock, 2022).

There is no doubt that lateral reading and other professional fact-checking strategies are essential to news media literacy. To develop these skills, it might take unlearning outdated evaluation strategies that are ineffective in the online spaces where we get our news and information.

Think like a journalist

Just as searching like a fact-checker is essential for verifying online news and information so is thinking like a journalist. Teaching students to think like a journalist is teaching them not only to critique news content but also to understand the nature of news and the codes and conventions that journalists apply to gather, assess, create, and present news and information. Thinking like a journalist provides a context for accessing, analyzing, evaluating and creating news content from the perspective of both the journalist and the news consumer.

In 2006 Stony Brook University began teaching one of the first college-level news literacy courses to undergraduate journalism majors and non-majors. The curriculum was designed and taught by journalists in consultation with librarians and faculty from psychology, philosophy, and political science. Stony Brook's Center for News Literacy's model focuses on teaching students how journalism works and developing their critical thinking skills to judge the reliability and credibility of news and information. Among the lessons are distinguishing journalism from other types of information, evaluating the evidence, credibility and reliability of news stories, differentiating between news and opinion journalism, identifying media and audience bias, and assessing the impact of digital technologies on news. The objective is to educate the next generation of news consumers to identify quality journalism and be informed and critical news readers, viewers and listeners in the digital age (Center for News Literacy, n.d.).

A case study (Fleming, 2014) of the Stony Brook program provides insight into the curriculum and its guiding principles and student response to this approach. Based on an evaluation of instructional documents, observation notes and interviews with students, faculty and administrators, students were highly engaged in the course content. They became more regular and skeptical news consumers and gained a multi-dimensional understanding of journalism. They were taught to access, evaluate and analyze the veracity of news, and to develop an appreciation of the work of journalists — which stresses verifiability, independence, and accountability — and the watchdog role and responsibility of the press in a democratic society. A more comprehensive assessment of the Stony Brook curriculum found that the emphasis on factual analysis was effective but lacked the connection to ideological, institutional and commercial forces that can influence news production (Fleming, 2015).

The effectiveness of the Stony Brook curriculum has also been assessed using a News Media Literacy Scale to compare students enrolled in the course with students who had not taken the course. As might be expected, news literacy students knew more about the news media system and current events and were more motivated to consume news after taking the course than students who had not taken the course (Maksl et al., 2017). What is unclear, however, is the extent to which the curriculum helps students establish lifelong news habits driven by factual analysis.

Another news literacy program started by a journalist is the News Literacy Project (NLP). Founded in 2008 as a national, nonpartisan nonprofit, NLP has become a leading educational program to teach middle and high school educators and their students the news consumer skills they need to critically navigate the digital media landscape and actively participate in civic life in a democracy. Its learning platform, called Checkology, is a virtual classroom that serves 250,000 students a year. According to NLP's key metrics, after completing the lessons a majority of students increased their news literacy comprehension in several areas: they can identify the standards of quality journalism, the purpose of propaganda, the five First Amendment freedoms and instances of journalism acting in a watchdog role of government, recognize bias in the news and examples of online posts that lack credible evidence, and express a sense of responsibility to check the veracity of information they share on social media (News Literacy Project, 2021).

Stony Brook's Center for News Literacy and the News Literacy Project created a foothold for news literacy education. Lessons and activities started popping up in middle and high schools and at universities, usually in journalism departments, as well as community programs and professional trainings, using a variety of formats and best practices but lacked consensus of learning objectives, key concepts and pedagogy (Fromm & O'Brien, 2016). When educators, researchers, and professional journalists convened at the 2014 National News Literacy Summit, the discussion and debate revealed a fragmented field with diverse voices and viewpoints and a variety of approaches to defining and conceptualizing news literacy. Some in the news literacy community questioned whether news literacy should be subsumed under media literacy, despite that media literacy educators have always taught it that way (Mihailidis, 2016).

A comprehensive report prepared for the National Association for Media Literacy Education, which was presented at its 2021 national conference, maps the direction of the field in the United States (Mihailidis et al., 2021). Based on an extensive review of the media literacy literature and in-depth interviews and surveys with media literacy educators, administrators and practitioners, researchers found that the call for implementing media literacy as a core educational standard is growing louder and more urgent after the political flashpoints of the January 6th insurrection on the U.S. Capitol and Black Lives Matter protests following the murder of George Floyd. The report underscores the importance of connecting media literacy practices to social inequities and the impact equitable-driven approaches to media literacy and news literacy can have in actualizing a vision of what democracy can be.

Although approaches and definitions of news literacy vary, most conceptualize news literacy as a subfield of media literacy focused on common civic goals that require an understanding of the nature of news, the conditions under which it is produced, and its unique role in a democracy. Some scholars prefer the term news media literacy to news literacy to stress that the media literacy framework is applied to news content (Maksl et al., 2017). No matter how it is defined or taught, news media literacy education is most effective when it focuses on factual awareness and analysis of news, and intersects media literacy, news literacy, civic responsibility and participation in democracy. The focus on facts is critical if we are to agree on factual truth based on credible and trustworthy news and information (Fleming & Karadjov, 2020).

The RAND Corporation's series of *Truth Decay* reports (Kavanagh & Rich, 2018; Huguet et al., 2019, 2021) highlight the key role that media literacy plays in developing news and digital literacy competencies to counter *"truth decay"* in the information ecosystem — the diminishing role of facts and analysis in American public life that threatens democracy. An extensive review of media literacy interventions and interviews with media literacy experts found that news and digital literacy is an increasingly important aspect of media literacy. RAND researchers conclude that media literacy is a viable strategy to target misinformation and disinformation that is blurring the line between fact and opinion and contributing to the crisis of news credibility and distrust in formerly respected purveyors of facts and objective standards of truth.

Many educators, researchers, and advocates are developing strategies to empower people of all ages, from children to seniors, with news literacy skills to spot false and misleading information and fact-check the evidence. We all have a responsibility to help prevent inaccurate, unreliable information and outright lies from spreading that can undermine our democracy. We need to consider if we are contributing to "truth decay." That means we need to be mindful of the way we consume, create and share news and information in the Digital Age of Disinformation.

Who Is a News Literate Person?

Identifying who is news literate is not that easy because news literacy is at the intersection of literacies. A news literate person is media literate, civic literate, digital and information literate. They know how to access, analyze, evaluate, and create media in all forms of communication. They follow the news on quality journalism outlets and are mindful of how and where they get their news. They can interpret what they see, hear and read like a journalist who understands the codes and conventions of the craft and values First Amendment guarantees. They can evaluate the reliability, credibility and trustworthiness of a source like a fact-checker who is skilled at reading laterally. They are aware of the social, political and economic effects of news media and can take action as informed citizens to protect the public's rights in a democracy. The concentric circles of news literacy illustrate the intersection of literacies in Figure 2.1.

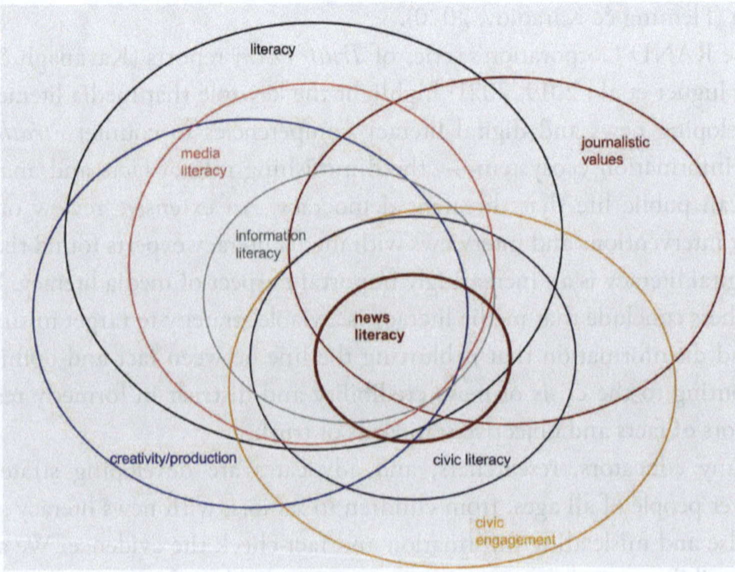

Fig. 2.1: Concentric Circles of News Literacy
Source: Reprinted by permission from Peter Levine, as cited in P. Mihailidis, 2014, Engagement Game Lab

Put simply: *A news literate person is aware of their own news habits, familiar with the way news is produced, distributed, and consumed, and has the ability to judge the credibility, reliability and relevance of news and information, distinguish between facts and opinion, identify bias and falsehoods, find quality and trustworthy journalism practices across media platforms, and understand and protect the vital role the First Amendment and a free press play in a democracy.*

"Struggling" to make sense of news

Based on the research, most people are not that news literate. The SHEG studies (Wineburg et al., 2020) use the word "struggle" to describe the majority of middle school, high school and college students' ability to evaluate even the most basic digital content. The researchers warn that not knowing how to identify credible information and trusted news sources impacts civic literacy and an informed citizenry and threatens a democracy.

In other studies, most adults surveyed admit they do not know that much about journalism or the First Amendment. According to a survey conducted by the American Press Institute (2018), the majority of respondents say it is not easy for them to distinguish news from opinion or a reporter from a columnist, especially in online news and social media. They are not sure what attribution means in journalism and are not familiar with certain terms such as native advertising. A Pew Research Center report (2020b) found that people were not confident in their ability to identify original sources of news and were not sure whether major news outlets do their own reporting. When it comes to knowledge about the First Amendment, the Freedom Forum's annual report (2021, 2022) on the state of the First Amendment consistently finds that the one right most people can recall is freedom of speech — but not that many know that the press is protected by the First Amendment as a check on the government for abuses of power and what that means. A news literate person should be familiar with the First Amendment and the core journalistic concepts and how to apply them to interpreting news. While journalism terms can be learned, even rote memorized, applying them is another matter.

Where Do We Go From Here?

We know from the research that people who are news literate tend to pay more attention to current events and are more inclined to vote and be civically engaged. We also know that most people, regardless of age, are not news literate and that may make them susceptible to believing rumors, hoaxes, conspiracy theories and other types of disinformation, especially if they get their news from social media. And we know that large-scale projects, such as the Stanford History Education Group, News Literacy Project, and Stony Brook's Center for News Literacy, are pioneering strategies to educate the next generation of news literate citizens.

We also know that media literacy provides a foundation upon which to build news literacy skills. Media literacy can better prepare us to access, analyze, evaluate, create, reflect and act on news content if it includes a basic understanding of journalism and the dynamics of the news-gathering process, the news media system, and the social, economic and political forces that influence the production and dissemination of news.

The Center for Media Literacy's (CML) framework was one of the first systematic methods for teaching and learning critical thinking skills for media literacy and has been widely adopted in the United States and internationally in schools, afterschool programs, universities, libraries, churches and community groups. CML defines media literacy according to the most commonly cited definition that was crafted at the 1992 Aspen Institute's National Leadership Conference on Media Literacy (Aufderheide, 1993): *the ability to access, analyze, evaluate and create media messages in a variety of forms.* Its evidence-based framework can be applied to any topic to impact knowledge, attitudes and behavior (Fingar & Jolls, 2019, 2013; Jolls & Johnsen, 2019). Over the years, I have used the CML framework to analyze a range of topics, from body image to cyberbullying to civic engagement. In this book, I apply CML's media literacy framework to provide a contextual understanding of the way news is produced, distributed, consumed, trusted and valued in society. The objective is to develop media literacy-driven critical thinking skills that build news literacy skills for the 21st century digital world.

An Integrative News Media Literacy Framework

The news media literacy framework explained in this book integrates CML's inquiry-driven pedagogy with news literacy concepts and web literacy strategies to deconstruct all forms of news products — whether it is a mainstream newspaper or newsmagazine, digital newspaper or newsletter, TV or cable newscast, talk radio, podcast, news app, social media or any other form of news. The starting point is the CML *Five Core Concepts and Key Questions* adapted to create a hybrid framework that integrates media literacy with news literacy and web literacy concepts to explore the nature of news and journalism practices and standards in the digital media ecosystem.

The CML framework is grounded in the *Empowerment Spiral* that can be applied to any media content. Based on the work of Brazilian educator Paolo Freire, the *Empowerment Spiral* identifies four steps to explain the process of inquiry for teaching and learning media literacy: Awareness, Analysis, Reflection and Action. Each step in this "Action Learning" model builds upon and reinforces the other to increase critical thinking, comprehension and the ability to make informed judgments. The Analysis step applies the *Five Key Questions* to analyze the author, format, content, audience, and purpose.

Empowerment Spiral

The Empowerment Spiral starts with an awareness of the issue that triggers the spiral of inquiry and analysis and, in turn, leads to reflection based on personal values and beliefs that empower taking action (adapted from Center for Media Literacy, n.d.):

- *Awareness:* Make a personal connection that generates "ah-ha" moments and opens a spiral of critical inquiry and exploration.
- *Analysis:* Apply the *Five Key Questions* to conduct a close analysis of the issue. Ask "what" and "how" questions such as "What's the evidence?" and "How credible is the source?" Avoid "why" questions because they can lead to personal interpretation and speculation that can disrupt the process of critical inquiry.
- *Reflection:* Go deeper by asking "So what?" or "What should we think or do based on the information?" Tap into your values, beliefs and worldview and consider ethical values, social justice or democratic principles such as First Amendment protections that guide individual and collective decision-making.
- *Action:* Learn by doing, individually or collectively. Decide how best to act based on your analysis and reflection. In this context, action does not mean *activism* or imply life-changing or world-altering action. Taking constructive action can be a simple action that symbolizes awareness. Or the action can be deciding not to take action.

Five Core Concepts and Five Key Questions

The *Five Core Concepts* and corresponding *Five Key Questions* guide a close analysis of the message and its creator, content, format, purpose, and the audience's interpretation of the message. The five core concepts are anchored in keywords (Center for Media Literacy, n.d.):

- *Keyword:* Authorship
  Core Concept: All media messages are constructed.
- *Keyword:* Format
  Core Concept: Media messages are constructed using a creative language with its own rules.
- *Keyword:* Audience
  Core Concept: Different people experience the same message differently.

- *Keyword:* Content
  Core Concept: Media have embedded values and points of view.
- *Keyword:* Purpose
  Core Concept: Most media messages are organized to gain profit and/or power.

For each keyword and core concept there is a key question for media consumers who deconstruct messages they receive and for content producers who construct messages they send. The media literacy framework with the keywords, core concepts and corresponding key questions for deconstruction and construction are outlined in Figure 2.2.

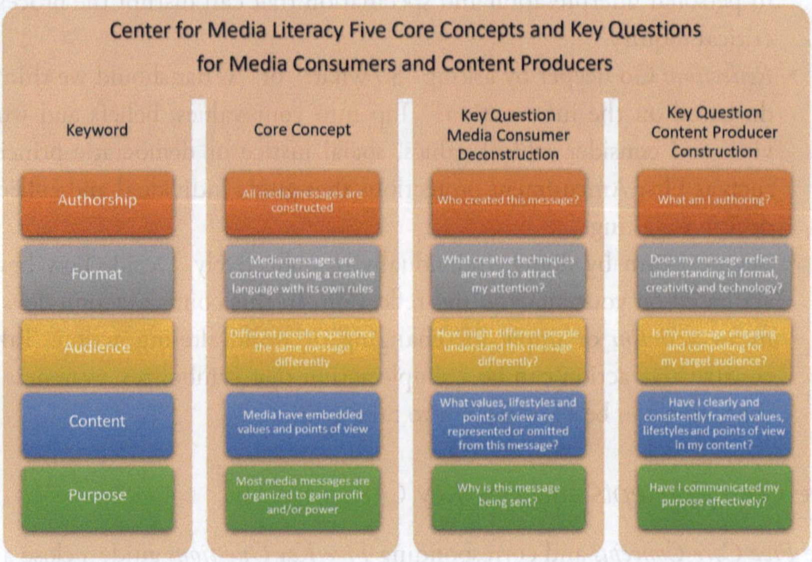

Fig. 2.2: Center for Media Literacy Framework
Source: Author/Center for Media Literacy (n.d.)

In the news media literacy framework, each core concept and key question is adapted for news messaging, and guiding questions are generated to assess and reflect on personal news habits, analyze news stories, and evaluate the news-gathering and production process and its influence on news consumers. The key questions incorporate concepts and terminology taught in university journalism courses and digital and news literacy programs. The goal is to gain news media knowledge while developing active and conscious news choices that empower the way we consume, create and share information in the digital world.

What's Next?

The next five chapters will help you closely "read" the news and think like a journalist. The starting point is to make sure we understand the purpose of news and can identify what is and what is not news. We encounter so many types of information in our daily lives, how do we know news when we come across it? In the Digital Age of Disinformation, knowing how to tell the difference between news and opinion or a factual news report and a conspiracy-driven story is an essential life skill.

References

American Press Institute. (2018). *Americans and the news media: What they do and don't understand about each other.* Media Insight Project. https://www.americanpressinstitute.org/publications/reports/survey-research/americans-and-the-news-media/

Aufderheide, P. (1993). *Media literacy: A report of the national leadership on media literacy.* Washington, D.C.: The Aspen Institute. https://files.eric.ed.gov/fulltext/ED365294.pdf

Baer, A., & Kipnis, D. (2020). Teaching lateral reading with an online tutorial: Preliminary study findings. *Library Scholarship, 27.* https://rdw.rowan.edu/lib_scholarship/27

Breakstone, J., Smith, M., Wineburg, S., Rapaport, A., Carle, J., Garland, M., & Saavedra, A. (2019). Students' civic online reasoning: A national portrait. Stanford History Education Group & Gibson Consulting. https://purl.stanford.edu/gf151tb4868

Breakstone, J., Smith, M., Connors, P., Ortega, T., Kerr, D., & Wineburg, S. (2021a). Lateral reading: College students learn to critically evaluate internet sources in an online course. *Harvard Kennedy School Misinformation Review, 2*(1). https://doi.org/10.37016/mr-2020-56

Breakstone, J., Smith, M., Wineburg, S., Rapaport, A., Carle, J., Garland, M., & Saavedra, A. (2021b). Students' civic online reasoning: A national portrait. *Educational Researcher, 20*(10), 1–11. https://doi.org/10.3102/0013189X211017495

Brodsky, J., Brooks, P., Scimeca, D., Todorova, R., Galati, P., Batson, M., Grosso, R., Matthews, M., Miller, V., & Caulfield, M. (2021, March). Improving college students' fact-checking strategies through lateral reading instruction in a general education civics course. *Cognitive Research Principles and Implications.* https://doi.org/10.1186/s41235-021-00291-4

Center for Media Literacy. (n.d.). Empowerment spiral. http://www.medialit.org/reading-room/empowerment-spiral

Center for Media Literacy. (n.d.). Five key questions form foundation for media literacy. http://www.medialit.org/reading-room/five-key-questions-form-foundation-media-inquiry

Center for News Literacy. (n.d.). What is news literacy? https://www.centerfornewsliteracy.org/what-is-news-literacy/

Craft, S., Ashley, S., & Maskl, A. (2017). News media literacy and conspiracy theory endorsement. *Communication and the Public, 2*(4), 388–401. https://journals.sagepub.com/doi/10.1177/2057047317725539

Fingar, K., & Jolls, T. (2013). Evaluation of a school-based violence prevention media literacy curriculum. *Injury Prevention: Journal of the International Society for Child and Adolescent Injury Prevention, 20*(3), 1–8. https://injuryprevention.bmj.com/content/20/3/183

Fingar, K., & Jolls, T. (2019). Evidence-based frameworks: Key to learning and scaling globally. In J. Tornero, G. Orozco & E. Hamburger (Eds.), *Media and information literacy in critical times: Reimagining learning and information environments,* (pp. 117–130) MILID Yearbook 2018–2019. UNESCO. http://www.gabinetecomunicacionyeducacion.com/sites/default/files/field/adjuntos/milidyearbook2018_19_.pdf

Fleming, J. (2014). Media literacy, news literacy or news appreciation? A case study of the news literacy program at Stony Brook University. *Journalism & Mass Communication Educator, 69(2), 145–165.* https://doi.org/10.1177/1077695813517885

Fleming, J. (2015). What do facts have to do with it? Exploring instructional emphasis in the Stony Brook news literacy curriculum. *Journal of Media Literacy Education, 7*(3), 73–92. https://digitalcommons.uri.edu/jmle/vol7/iss3/6

Fleming, J., & Karadjov, C. (2020). Focusing on facts: Media and news literacy education in the age of misinformation. In W. Christ & B. DeAbreu (Eds.), *Media literacy in a disruptive media environment,* (pp. 77–93). Routledge.

Freedom Forum. (2021). *The First Amendment: Where America stands.* https://survey.freedomforum.org/content/uploads/2021/09/Freedom-Forum-Downloadable-Report.pdf

Freedom Forum. (2022, June). *2022 Update: First Amendment sparks and could bridge divide.* https://survey.freedomforum.org/2022-update/

Fromm, M., & O'Brien, C. (2016). Finding consensus: A pilot survey in news literacy education. *Journalism Education, 5*(1), 123–135. https://www.academia.edu/27138511/Exploring_News_Literacy_Preparing_future_journalists_and_citizens_for_engagement_in_global_digital_culture

Guess, A., Nagler, J., & Tucker, J. (2019, January). Less than you think: Prevalence and predictors of fake news dissemination on Facebook. *Science Advances 5*(1). https://www.science.org/doi/10.1126/sciadv.aau4586?cookieSet=1

Huguet, A., Kavanagh, J., Baker, G., & Blumenthal, M. (2019). *Countering truth decay: Exploring media literacy education as a tool for mitigating truth decay.* RAND Corporation. https://www.rand.org/pubs/research_reports/RR3050.html

Huguet, A., Kavanagh, J., Baker, G., Hamilton, L., & Pane, J. (2021). *Media literacy standards to counter truth decay.* RAND Corporation. https://doi.org/10.7249/RRA112-12

Jolls, T., & Johnsen, M. (2019). Media literacy: A foundational skill for democracy in the 21st century. *Hastings Law Journal, 69*(5), Article 4. https://repository.uchastings.edu/hastings_law_journal/vol69/iss5/4

Kavanagh, J., & Rich, M. (2018). *Truth decay. An initial exploration of the diminishing role of facts and analysis in American public life.* RAND Corporation. https://www.rand.org/pubs/research_reports/RR2314.html

Maksl, A., Craft, S., Ashley, S., & Miller, D. (2017). The usefulness of a news media literacy measure in evaluating a news literacy curriculum. *Journalism & Mass Communication Educator, 72*(2), 228–241.

McGrew, S. (2020). Learning to evaluate: An intervention in civic online reasoning. *Computers and Education, 145*. https://doi.org/10.1016/j.compedu.2019.103711

McGrew, S., Smith, M., Breakstone, J., Ortega, T., Wineburg, S. (2019). Improving university students' web savvy: An intervention study. *British Journal of Educational Psychology, 89*(3), 489–500.

Mihailidis, P. (2014). Seeking coherence: Reflections on the National News Literacy Summit. Engagement Game Lab. https://engagementgamelab.wordpress.com/2014/09/28/seeking-coherence-reflections-on-the-national-news-literacy-summit/

Mihailidis, P. (2016). Exploring news literacy: Preparing future journalists and citizens for engagement in global digital culture. *Journalism Education, 5*(1), 11–13. https://journalism-education.org/wp-content/uploads/2020/07/Intro.pdf

Mihailidis, P., Ramasubramanian, S., Tully, M., Bhusari, B., Johnson, P., & Riewestahl, E. (2021). Equity and impact in media literacy practice: Mapping the field in the United States. National Association for Media Literacy Education. https://mappingimpactfulml.org

Moore, R., & Hancock, J. (2022). A digital media literacy intervention for older adults improves resilience to fake news. *Scientific Report, 12*. https://doi.org/10.1038/s41598-022-08437-0

News Literacy Project. (2021). *Summary of assessment results: The Checkology virtual classroom 2020–2021.*

Pavlounis, D., Johnston, J., Brodsky, J., & Brooks, P. (2021, November). The digital media literacy gap: How to build widespread resilience to false and misleading information using evidence-based classroom tools. *CIVIX Canada*. https://ctrl-f.ca/en/wp-content/uploads/2022/01/The-Digital-Media-Literacy-Gap.pdf

Pew Research Center. (2020a). *Americans who mainly get their news on social media are less engaged, less knowledgeable.* https://www.journalism.org/2020/07/30/americans-who-mainly-get-their-news-on-social-media-are-less-engaged-less-knowledgeable/

Pew Research Center. (2020b). *Many Americans are unsure whether sources of news do their own reporting.* https://www.pewresearch.org/fact-tank/2020/12/08/many-americans-are-unsure-whether-sources-of-news-do-their-own-reporting/

Pew Research Center. (2021). *How Americans navigated the news in 2020: A tumultuous year in review.* https://www.journalism.org/2021/02/22/how-americans-navigated-the-news-in-2020-a-tum ultuous-year-in-review/

Stanford History Education Group. (n.d.). Civic Online Reasoning. https://cor.stanford.edu/

Truth Check. (n.d.). Truth Check toolkit for community and influencer engagement. https://thetruthcheck.org/

Wineburg, S., McGrew, S., Breakstone, J., & Ortega, T. (2016). *Evaluating information: The cornerstone of civic online reasoning.* Stanford Digital Repository. http://purl.stanford.edu/fv75 1yt5934

Wineburg, S., Breakstone, J., Ziv, N., & Smith, M. (2020). *Educating for misunderstanding: How approaches to teaching digital literacy make students susceptible to scammers, rogues, bad actors, and hate mongers.* Working Paper A-21322, Stanford History Education Group, Stanford University. https://purl.stanford.edu/mf412bt5333

Wineburg, S., Breakstone, J., McGrew, S., Smith, M., & Ortega, T. (2022). Lateral reading on the open Internet: A district-wide field study in high school government classes. *Journal of Educational Psychology, 114*(5). https://psycnet.apa.org/fulltext/2022-53872-001.html

3 What Is News?

News is one of those things that you think you know the definition until you are asked to define it. There are numerous definitions of news offered by media scholars and journalism professionals. Underlying them all is the notion that news is about something important happening now that people need to know and is based on facts. Here is a basic definition synthesized from several different ones: *News is a timely report based on facts gathered by a news organization — newspaper, TV and radio newscasts, news magazine, news agency, digital and online news outlet — that helps us make sense of our world and form opinions about current affairs that are relevant to us.*

Local news informs us about what is happening in our community, national news reports events and issues affecting the country, and international news covers stories occurring around the world. Whatever the news is about, it is based on facts and not opinion. A *fact* is observable and verifiable information based on evidence. An *opinion* is a personal point of view that may or may not be based on facts. Both news and opinion are forms of journalism that help us understand the world.

The nature of news is much more complex than any definition. To fully understand what news is, we need to consider the purpose of news, how news differs from other types of information, and why journalism is the only media practice that is protected by the U.S. Constitution.

What Is the Purpose of News?

While most media, even news media, are profit-driven, the primary purpose of news is to establish truth and inform citizens about what is happening in the world in order to empower them to participate responsibly in democracy.

When we think of news, we probably think of front-page stories about politics, the economy or crime. What about a personality profile about a celebrity, or an investigative piece about cheating in sports, or a feature about the top 10 places to live in the United States, or consumer tips about the latest tech trends? Are these also considered news? All of these are news, just different types of stories. Think of news on a continuum, from hard to soft. The purpose is the same, which is to inform, but the tone and writing styles differ.

What is the difference between hard news and soft news?

Hard news stories are up-to-the-minute factual accounts of what happened or is happening or about to happen, why it happened, and how people, especially the news audience, might be affected. It is a story with immediacy such as a policy change, election outcome, virus outbreak, contaminated food, crime, war, the economy, protest rally, speech, court testimony, catastrophe or natural disaster such as a plane or train crash, explosion, fire, flood or earthquake. If the event is happening right now, it is called "breaking news."

Soft news are stories that do not have the same immediacy as hard news. These stories are feature stories that focus on a person, place or issue, or offer useful information such as consumer tips or advice about a topic that readers find interesting. The story might be about entertainment, the arts, lifestyles, or a human-interest angle of a hard news story written in a compelling way.

How is news different from other types of information?

We encounter different types of information every day — news, opinion, propaganda, entertainment, advertising, publicity, and user-generated content on social media. News and opinion are different forms of journalism. *News* keeps us informed about issues and events happening in the world and about newsmakers

— people of interest or importance in the news — while *opinion* offers a point of view about an issue that helps us make a judgment or decide what action to take.

Unlike news and opinion journalism, which are evidence-based and strive for accuracy and truth, these other types of information focus more on profit and power. *Propaganda* is promoted by political strategists who use tactics such as fear, flattery, name-calling and power plays that distort information to manipulate emotions and build mass support to gain power. *Entertainment* media's goal is to create content that amuses, pleases and diverts audiences in order to make money for production companies, social media platforms, social media influencers, actors, musicians, and other performers. The purpose of *advertising* is to sell a product or service, while the goal of *publicity* is to raise awareness and promote a client's brand or cause. The newest type of information is raw, unfiltered, unedited and unverified *user-generated* self-expression on social media created by anyone with access to the Internet.

It is not always easy to distinguish among the different types of information because they borrow techniques from one another to attract audiences, increase profits, even intentionally deceive the public with content mistaken for news. Journalism appropriates entertainment and advertising techniques to connect with audiences and compete for ratings and revenue. Advertising, publicity and propaganda use journalism formats to make their messages appear more credible. Entertainment borrows from journalism in late-night talk show formats that typically structure the monologue around the news of the day, and movies and TV shows oftentimes ground storytelling in real news events to make the drama more provocative and occasionally feature news anchors as characters playing themselves.

Although the lines between journalism and other types of information can be blurred, remember that each one has a distinct purpose and uses certain methods to achieve its desired outcome. Some educators categorize the types of information into neighborhoods or zones. Whatever the label, sorting information into groups helps to recognize how each type of information is different from one another. These differences are fundamental to understanding the role of journalism in society and distinguishing news from entertainment, advertising, propaganda, publicity, and user-generated content on social media. Keep in mind that sometimes information may look like news, read and sound like news, but it is not news. It is simply disguised as news.

How might another type of information be mistaken for news?

In the media culture where the different types of information are inherently intertwined, it is not that hard to mistake journalism for another type of information. News can look like entertainment and entertainment can look like news. News can be confused with advertising, publicity, propaganda, and user-created content on social media. A good example is advertising that can be mistaken for news.

When we go online we may see what looks like a news article or news clip about a medical breakthrough for building muscle and reducing fat. Click it on and the information may be very interesting, but the main purpose is to sell us a product. How could we know? Check carefully for the label "ad" or "sponsored content." Sponsored content is a type of ad called native advertising or advertorial. *Native advertising* matches the format of the media platform where it appears, and an *advertorial* — which blends two words, advertisement and editorial — is an ad that is made to look like editorial content, such as a news article, opinion piece or video segment.

Another example is a *video news release* or VNR that is part of a newscast. A VNR is a pre-packaged video segment designed to look like a news story, but it is not created by a news outlet and usually lacks transparency. VNRs are produced by ad agencies and public relations specialists to shape public opinion or drive brand awareness of their client's service or product. The segment might feature interviews with experts and people who say they use and benefit from the product. They may be actors and not actually who they say they are, but that is not entirely the point. The intention is to mistake the VNR for a news story, produced by the news outlet where it appears, and not see it as the promotional piece it really is. What should we look for? Verified claims, authoritative sources, identified locations, and reporting by a journalist employed by that news outlet. If these are missing, then it just may be a VNR.

What Makes News Reliable?

The reliability of news is inherent in the craft of journalism, its ethical codes of conduct, the transparency of the news-gathering process, and the watchdog role that the press serves in our democracy (Kovach & Rosenstiel, 2021). Here are three things to know about journalism that makes news reliable.

Three things to know about journalism

Journalists are trained media professionals grounded in ethical codes of conduct.

Journalism requires specialized knowledge and skills and an adherence to ethical behavior that is grounded in professional codes of conduct. Many people do not realize that writing a news story and calling oneself a journalist does not make one a journalist. Journalists have training in the editorial process and ethical decision-making fundamental to journalism, and take responsibility for the information they provide, regardless of the medium in which they work. Professional associations and individual news organizations provide standards for codes of conduct to evaluate journalists' ethical behavior.

Journalism standards are grounded in core principles of *truthfulness, accuracy, independence, impartiality, fairness, public accountability, and minimize harm.* Journalists are obligated to tell the truth and not use information deceptively. Journalists strive to be accurate and fact-based. To act independently free of personal and financial conflicts of interest. To be impartial without bias and prejudice. To be fair and balanced and include all credible sides to a story. To be transparent and accountable to their readers, viewers and listeners. To balance the public's need for information against potential harm to sources, colleagues, and the public.

News organizations make their professional codes available to the public, usually on their websites, and revise them as the changing media ecosystem impacts journalistic practices. A few examples are the Society of Professional Journalists Code of Ethics (2014), the Radio Television Digital News Association Code of Ethics (2015), and Associated Press Statement of News Values and Principles (n.d.). If a news outlet does not allow public access to their codes of conduct, then think twice about the trustworthiness of that news outlet and the information it distributes.

Journalism is a discipline of verification.

The practice of journalism is subject to a transparent news-gathering process that is verifiable, independent, and accountable or VIA. (The acronym VIA was coined by the Center for News Literacy at Stony Brook University Digital Resource Center, n.d.)

Information must be verifiable. Journalists verify facts and establish where their facts come from, explain what they know and do not know and what information might be contradictory and why.

Journalists must be free of conflicts of interest related to the story they are reporting. Journalists reveal any personal or financial conflicts of interest concerning their relationship to the news source or the story.

Journalists are accountable for their work. Journalists sign their name to their work and take responsibility for its accuracy, and if they make an error, correct it publicly. Political polls and surveys also require transparency disclosing who conducted the poll or survey, how it was conducted and who participated, and whether the results are within the margin of error.

VIA is an indicator of the reliability of a news story. If the accuracy of the information can be confirmed by multiple sources, if there is no conflict of interest among the journalist, news source and story, and if the journalist or news organization stands behind the story, corrects any errors and takes responsibility for its truthfulness, then the story is reliable. If one of these is missing, then the information may not be reliable (see Figure 3.1)

Fig. 3.1: Is the News Story Reliable?
Source: Author

The press is protected by the First Amendment to the U.S. Constitution. A free press is guaranteed by the First Amendment because the news media's role is to assure an informed citizenry in a democracy. Without First Amendment guarantees of the right to a free press, citizens may not get reliable, credible, and accurate information they need to actively and responsibly participate in a democracy. The First Amendment states:

> Congress shall make no law respecting an establishment of religion, or prohibiting the free exercise thereof; or abridging the freedom of speech, or of the press; or the right of the people peaceably to assemble, and to petition the Government for a redress of grievances.

Who exactly is *the press?* We refer to the collection of news media organizations and the journalists who work for them to deliver news to the public as *the press.* The press includes print and digital newspapers and news magazines, TV and radio broadcast news stations, cable news outlets, news agencies, and online news sites. Another name for the press is the Fourth Estate.

What Is the Fourth Estate?

The *Fourth Estate* refers to the vital role the press serves in a democracy as an unofficial fourth branch of government monitoring the legislative, judicial and executive branches for abuses of power. First Amendment protections enable the press to operate without excessive government interference in order to uncover truths and hold government and institutions accountable to the public. The press as the Fourth Estate acts as democracy's watchdog providing newsworthy and trustworthy information citizens need to make informed decisions about political and social issues. In turn, citizens have a responsibility to keep informed in order to actively and responsibly participate in democracy. The relationship between the First Amendment, the Fourth Estate, and the citizens is illustrated in Figure 3.2.

When the First Amendment was adopted in 1791, the Framers of the Constitution could not foresee the evolution of the press from newspapers to radio and TV broadcast and cable news to digital news and social networks. Today the guarantee of a free press encompasses all news media technologies that together produce a glut of real news along with disinformation.

Other contributors to this information glut are self-organizing online communities and networked individuals who seek alternatives to mainstream media outside of the Fourth Estate. They are bloggers, civic leaders, citizen journalists, activists, nonprofits, along with individuals and groups on political and social forums who participate in the emergent Fifth Estate.

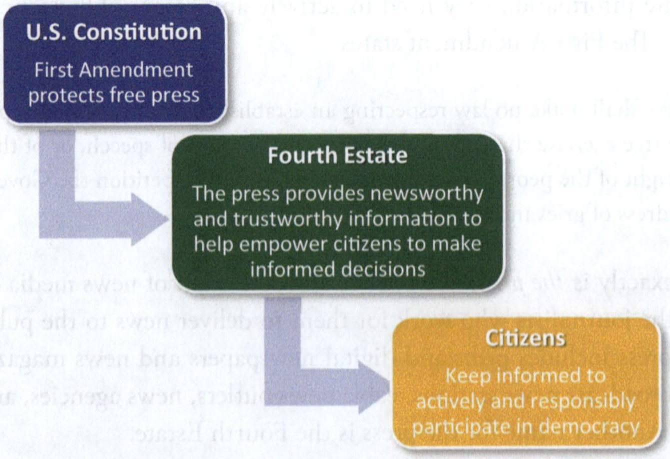

Fig. 3.2: The Fourth Estate
Source: Author

Do you know your First Amendment rights?

If you are like most Americans, the answer is no, not really. Most Americans believe the First Amendment is vital, but they do not know much about the rights it guarantees them — that is according to the Freedom Forum's annual survey (2022, 2021) that tracks the state of the First Amendment. Without being prompted, some people cannot name any of the five rights the First Amendment guarantees, while others can name a few. Still others are incorrect about what rights it protects. Some mistakenly think that the right to bear arms and the right to vote are protected under the First Amendment.

The one protection that most can recall is freedom of speech, followed by religion. Americans value the right to express themselves and to worship any way they want, but they are not sure exactly how the rights apply and are divided about how these rights should be regulated. Most know that hate speech is protected but some think it should not be, and a majority believe that false claims made by politicians are not protected but they are. Divisions about the role of religion are deepening with a majority of people feeling that religious freedom, especially Christian beliefs, is being threatened — nearly a third incorrectly believe that the Constitution specifies that the United States is a Christian nation. When it comes to the right to petition the government, not many people can name the right, even though many have signed a petition. Very few can name the freedom to peacefully assemble, and while most have not participated in a march, rally or protest, they believe the right is necessary for a healthy democracy.

Freedom of the press presents a dilemma. On the one hand, people think that "fake news" is a real problem, media should act as a watchdog for government, and social media should be held responsible for allowing false or misleading information to be posted on its platform. On the other hand, they do not consider a free press as one of the most essential freedoms, are mixed about whether the press is doing a good job as a watchdog but think journalists deserve special legal protection from harm, and are skeptical of journalists because of a perceived bias. Some even view journalists as a threat to the First Amendment and would consider limiting press and speech to combat the problem of mis/disinformation. This is not surprising because the press is under constant attack, especially by political figures who have referred to the press as "the enemy of the people." Calling quality news organizations the people's enemy is far from the truth and is really about politicians calling out journalists for saying something negative about them when journalists are merely holding politicians accountable for their actions. At a time when Americans are politically divided and uncertain about how First Amendment rights are exercised, many express optimism that the country can bridge the divisions and that the First Amendment is a way to do that.

What Is the Fifth Estate?

The *Fifth Estate* refers to the public common that is created by the Internet and empowered by social networks. This digital space enables networked individuals to circumvent mainstream gatekeepers to get their voices heard. In certain ways, the Fifth Estate has decentralized power by placing it directly in the hands of the people who can hold the mainstream media, politicians and government accountable, challenge the influence of institutional authority, and facilitate political and social movements. This Internet-enabled platform is a place where a broad spectrum of views co-exists that represent the left, right and center, from mainstream positions to outlier perspectives and subversive activities. While the Fifth Estate is diverse, it can also be divisive.

Who is part of the Fifth Estate? Originally, the Fifth Estate was comprised primarily of bloggers on the Internet. As social networks developed and people increasingly used digital devices to connect and communicate on social media, the Fifth Estate expanded to include these networked individuals and groups. It includes anyone who writes a blog, tweets or retweets, posts comments, shares photos, uploads videos, starts a petition, organizes a fundraiser, advocates for a cause, rates a product, contributes to a wiki, purports to be a social media influencer, participates in citizen journalism, crowdsourcing or other non-mainstream news activity, as well as journalists who publish outside of traditional news outlets. No matter what their views are, the Fifth Estate enhances their communication capacity by giving them a powerful platform on which to voice their viewpoints and potentially shape news and policy decisions as well as personal attitudes and opinions (Dutton, 2009).

The Fifth Estate has become a dynamic digital space that is shaped by the way we use the Internet, how the Internet and social media are regulated, and the emergence of new ways to network online. It is an alternative sphere of influence that does not depend on traditional mass media, is not obliged to employ transparent news-gathering guidelines that are verifiable, independent and accountable or practice ethical codes of conduct required by the Fourth Estate. Depending on how it is used, the Fifth Estate can be a tool for a more vibrant democracy or for an autocracy or anarchy. That means the Fifth Estate can be a fertile breeding ground for "fake news," conspiracy theories, hoaxes, pseudoscience, doxxing, and other types of disinformation.

What Is "Fake News"?

If news is based on facts, then "fake news" must not be. This is not entirely correct.

"Fake news" is fraudulent news. False news. Fictitious news. Fabricated news. *"Fake news"* refers to inaccurate or untrue news reports that are intentionally constructed to mislead the public and tend to be politically or ideologically motivated. In the 21st century, "fake news" is usually circulated on the Internet, especially on social media. The term "fake news" has been appropriated by politicians and other powerful people to characterize factual news that they do not like or disagree with because it is unfavorable or critical of them. Instead of allowing news to publicly discredit them, they attempt to discredit the news itself by calling it "fake news" because the news story could potentially harm their reputation, sully their record, reveal a scandalous liaison or illegal activity or worse.

Labeling news as "fake news" when it is real news has created confusion about what is fact and what is fiction, and which sources are reliable and trustworthy and which ones are not. Using the term "fake news" as a buzzword for any type of misinformation or disinformation further confounds the issue. The media landscape is more complex than a term that implies there are two types of news, fake or real. Several people have proposed to retire the term because it has been overused, misused, co-opted by politicians, is limited to news, means something different to different people, and essentially has become meaningless. What we really need is a new vocabulary to better understand how to identify and counteract the tactics, intent and impact of misinformation and disinformation in the ever-evolving media ecosystem.

Since the term "fake news" is widely used as a catchall for misinformation and disinformation and there is no alternative word at this time, "fake news" appears in quotes in this book to signal that the term itself is misleading because it does not denote what it claims to mean (Garber, 2016). Here are three things to know about the nature of "fake news."

Three things to know about "fake news"

The term "fake news" is an oxymoron.

The term "fake news" combines two words that are contradictory. The word "news" refers to a factual report of an event, while the word "fake" means untrue, counterfeit or falsified. Using the word "fake" as an adjective to describe news is incongruous because a news story is expected to a be a true and verifiable account of a real event. By labeling news as fake, even when it is true, has contributed to making facts a partisan issue, undermining trust in journalism, and invalidating the credibility of a news outlet. Nevertheless, the term "fake news" has made its way into the dictionary, legitimizing the expression.

Lexicographers track how words spread and will add a word that is frequently used in order to update a dictionary. After the 2016 U.S. presidential election, the use of the term "fake news" became popularized and more widespread. According to *Collins Dictionary*, the term increased in use 365 percent in one year, prompting them to name "fake news" the 2017 word-of-the-year and add the word to its print edition (Associated Press, 2017; Collins Dictionary, 2017). *Oxford English Dictionary*, a standard-bearer of lexicographers, officially recognized the term in 2019 and added it to its lexicon (Oxford English Dictionary, 2019). One notable exception to adding "fake news" to its dictionary is *Merriam-Webster*. They have no plans to add the term because they contend that the meaning is a self-explanatory compound noun — "fake news" is news that is fake (Merriam Webster, n.d.).

Comparing different dictionary definitions of "fake news" reveals two dimensions: factivity and intention. There is a general consensus that "fake news" is false, intentionally misleading, and usually promotes a particular agenda. For example, *Collins Dictionary* defines "fake news" as "false, often sensational, information disseminated under the guise of news reporting" (Collins Dictionary, n.d.). *Oxford English Dictionary* defines the term as "news that conveys or incorporates false, fabricated, or deliberately misleading information, or that is characterized as or accused of doing so" (Oxford English Dictionary, n.d.). The *Cambridge Dictionary* definition is "false stories that appear to be news, spread on the internet or using other media, usually created to influence political views or as a joke" (Cambridge Dictionary, n.d.). The go-to online reference *Dictionary.com* defines "fake news" as "false news stories, often of a sensational nature, created to be widely shared or distributed for the purpose of generating revenue, or promoting or discrediting a public figure, political movement, company, etc." (Dictionary.com, n.d.).

"Fake News" is not new to journalism.

While the term "fake news" became widespread during the 2016 Trump campaign and presidency, its roots date back to Colonial America. When the Founding Fathers were forging a new nation, they relied on false news reports to influence public opinion to advance their cause. Some of the more notable instances occurred around efforts to mobilize support among the colonists for the American Revolution.

For example, in 1769, John Adams wrote in his diary about conspiring with other Boston patriots to fabricate stories to undercut British authority in Massachusetts: "The Evening spent in preparing for the Next Days Newspaper - a curious Employment. Cooking up Paragraphs, Articles, Occurences, &c. -- working the political Engine!" (Adams Family Papers, 1769). In 1782, while serving as the American ambassador to France, Benjamin Franklin concocted a story about Native Americans scalping colonists and sending the scalps to King George for his pleasure in order to create anti-Indian sentiment and undermine British authority in the colonies. Franklin published a fake edition of a real Boston newspaper to circulate the story and sent copies to his colleagues to spread it widely in other newspapers (Parkinson, 2016).

By the 1830s, as literacy became more widespread, newspapers emerged as the first true mass medium. This period of journalism is known as the Penny Press because newspapers cost one cent and became an affordable source of information for working and middle-class people. To appeal to the audience and turn a profit, newspapers covered true crime, scandals, celebrity news, sensational stories, and hoaxes to increase circulation. One of the most infamous examples is "The Great Moon Hoax." In 1835, the *New York Sun,* one of the largest circulating newspapers at the time, published a six-part series entitled "Great Astronomical Discoveries Lately Made," which claimed there was an alien civilization on the moon and even cited a renowned British astronomer (McQueen, 2018).

The Penny Press paved the way in the 1890s for Yellow Journalism, a style of newspaper reporting notorious for emphasizing sensationalism over facts for profit. Yellow Journalism is known for using bold headlines, scare tactics, cartoons and color, reporting rumors and fabricating facts to attract readers. The term "Yellow Journalism" originated out of the rivalry between Joseph Pulitzer, publisher of the *New York World*, and William Randolph Hearst, publisher of the *New York Journal*, and their competitive profit-driven tactics to outsell the other. The incident that gave rise to the term Yellow Journalism involved a popular cartoon strip called "Hogan's Alley" that was illustrated with the color yellow and featured a character called the Yellow Kid. The cartoon character became so well-known, and sold so many newspapers, that Hearst hired the cartoonist away from Pulitzer. Pulitzer retaliated by hiring a new cartoonist to continue the same cartoon in his newspaper.

The peak of Yellow Journalism came in 1898 when the circulation war between Hearst and Pulitzer contributed to swaying public opinion in support of the Spanish-American War. Some even credit Hearst's self-promotion tactics to inciting the war. A legendary exchange between Hearst and a reporter he sent to Cuba to illustrate the war captures the essence of Yellow Journalism and "fake news." When the reporter cabled Hearst saying there was no war to cover and he wanted to return home, Hearst allegedly replied, "Please remain. You furnish the pictures, and I'll furnish the war" (McQueen, 2018, p. 27).

The legacy of Yellow Journalism is alive and well in today's infodemic of alternative facts, fraudulent news, and misleading information that deliberately misinforms the public. However, 21st century "fake news" is in a different category from earlier forms because technology has emboldened it as a tool of mass production and distribution across media platforms. In the modern media ecosystem, "fake news" is ubiquitous, spreads at lightning speed, its influence is pervasive, and it is highly profitable. Anyone can create it, not just news publishers, and people are likely to fall for "fake news" because it is intermixed with real news on news aggregators and social media sites, which require fact-checking that most people do not do. People also tend to believe "fake news" that comes with an implicit or explicit endorsement from family, friends and social media communities when they like, share, retweet and tag it, multiplying its reach. Studies show that leading up to the 2016 U.S. presidential election there was more engagement with "fake news" stories on social media than with factual news stories from mainstream news outlets. This number almost tripled during the 2020 U.S. presidential election, especially with sites rated politically "extreme" (Edelson et al., 2021; Goldstein, 2021).

"Fake news" is a very real problem that has weaponized news and information against the press, journalists, and democracy. This is best summed up by a quote in a NewseumED exhibit on the topic: "Politicians around the world call legitimate journalism that is critical of them 'fake news.' Some repressive regimes use it as an excuse to jail reporters — undermining the role of the press and fanning mistrust of journalists. At the same time, false information deceptively presented as legitimate news and spread online has become a powerful troubling force in the world" (NewseumED, 2019).

"Fake News" is disinformation.

"Fake news" is not simply misinformation — it is intentional misinformation that is purposefully produced and disseminated, otherwise known as disinformation. The difference between misinformation and disinformation is *intent*. Misinformation is false or inaccurate information spread unintentionally without malice, whereas disinformation is false information spread intentionally to mislead, deceive, or obscure the truth. Intent is also central to another type of disinformation called malinformation (Wardle & Derakhshan, 2018).

One of the more common types of *misinformation* results from covering a breaking news story. In the urgency to get the news out, some information may be incomplete or unknowingly inaccurate but will be corrected by the news organization as more facts become known. Misinformation can also result from reporting errors such as misspelling a name, misidentifying a photo caption, misreporting a date or statistic, a translation mistake by an interpreter, a rumor that circulates before it is disproven, or when satire is taken seriously. Social media users who do not know the information is incorrect might share it, but not with the intent to cause harm.

Unlike misinformation, the purpose of *disinformation* is to deliberately confuse or mislead the public, influence public opinion, or cause harm to a person, social group, organization, institution, or even a country for political, financial, social, psychological or emotional motivations. The information might be entirely fabricated, or based on a kernel of truth, or stripped of context to support the intended message, or intentionally manipulated using audio and/or video editing techniques. The source creating and disseminating the disinformation either is a true believer or knows it is false and tries to get others to share it widely to amplify the impact. Social media users might knowingly circulate rumors, hoaxes and conspiracy theories or unwittingly spread them because they did not check the veracity of the information.

Another type of information created with a harmful intent is *malinformation*. This is the deliberate publication of private information for the purpose of inflicting harm on a person, group, company or institution rather than serving the public interest. It might involve changing the context, date, time or place of the actual content. *Doxxing* is a form of malinformation that involves publishing identifying information without the person's permission such as disclosing their full name, address, telephone number, workplace or sexual orientation, or posting photos including revenge porn, or leaking the content of emails. The key role that intent plays in misinformation, disinformation and malinformation is illustrated in Figure 3.3.

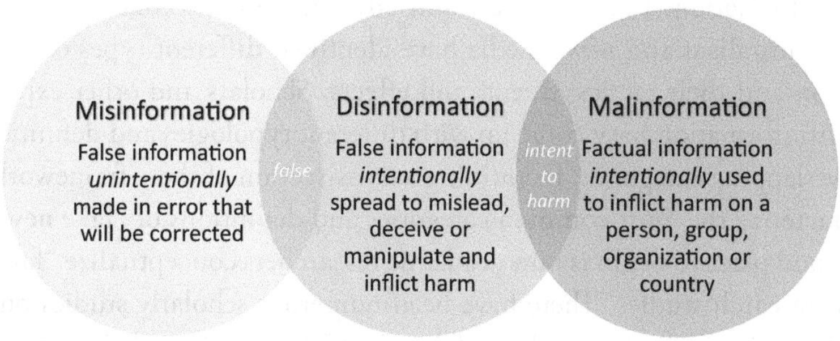

Fig. 3.3: Information Intent
Source: Author

Do people understand what "fake news" is?

Most people do not recognize the difference between misinformation and disinformation or understand what is meant by "fake news." They tend to equate reporting errors by an established news organization, which are made in good-faith and are correctable, with the deliberate deception of fabricated news stories circulating on social media, and with politicians discrediting verified but negative news reports they don't like.

When "fake news" was beginning to inundate the news cycle around the 2016 U.S. presidential election, Pew Research Center (2016) conducted a survey that revealed two-thirds of American adults felt that fraudulent news stories were causing confusion about which basic facts to believe and one-quarter said they had shared a fabricated story. In another survey conducted by Gallup/Knight Foundation, most Americans said it is harder to keep well-informed, struggle to find objective news, and generally do not agree on how to define "fake news" (Knight Foundation, 2018).

Admittedly, it can be confusing distinguishing between misinformation and disinformation, plus the term "fake news" does not capture the complexities of the different types of fraudulent stories clamoring for attention in the media ecosystem.

What are different types of "fake news"?

What exactly is meant by "fake news"? Is satire "fake news"? A conspiracy theory? A hoax? A partisan news site? There is no consensus about what constitutes "fake news." Libraries have created guides to "fake news" and misinformation and disinformation. Public interest and advocacy groups concerned about the state of journalism and news media have identified different types of mis/disinformation and their tactics, intent, and effects. Scholars and other experts who study disinformation have come up with different typologies and definitions that have overlapping categories. Examining a cross-section of these frameworks helps to characterize the most common categories and definitions of "fake news."

A good place to begin is how academic researchers conceptualize "fake news" in their research studies. There have been numerous scholarly studies published in academic journals that analyze "fake news." In a review of these studies, six different categories of "fake news" were identified based on the degree to which the type of "fake news" relies on facts and its intent to mislead or deceive: satire, parody, fabrication, manipulation, advertising, and propaganda. What these types of "fake news" have in common is that they appear to look and feel like real news. It may be that an article is written to read like a genuine news article, or a website is constructed to look like an authentic website, or native advertising appropriates characteristics of real advertising, or a photo includes attributions to make it look realistic (Tandoc et al., 2017).

First Draft, a nonpartisan nonprofit coalition whose mission is to protect and empower communities from harmful misinformation, developed a typology that divides the information ecosystem into seven categories of mis/disinformation based on three elements: content that is created and shared, motivations for creating the content, and ways the content is disseminated. The seven categories are: satire or parody, misleading content, imposter content, fabricated content, false connection, false context, and manipulated content. The motivations for creating the content are mapped against one another to analyze the specific purpose of its intent to deceive the public: poor journalism, parody, passion, partisanship, profit, political influence, or propaganda (First Draft, 2019).

The News Literacy Project, a nonpartisan national education nonprofit, provides programs and resources for educators to help students develop skills to discern fact from fiction and actively participate in democracy. They use the First Draft categories as a jumping off point to create a five-fold typology of mis/disinformation: satire, false context, imposter content, manipulated content, and fabricated content (News Literacy Project, n.d.).

Another framework developed by Pen America, a group whose mission is to unite writers and defend and protect the freedom to write, defines four categories of fraudulent news content. They distinguish between stories written, financed or disseminated by people or groups for the purpose of profit, especially from online advertising; political motives in support of a candidate, party or ideology; state-affiliated objectives, usually government-sponsored misinformation; and spreading conspiracy theories because they genuinely believe the fabricated story. In their report about fraudulent news, Pen America explains that they do not consider satire, mistakes, hyper-partisan news and commentary, clickbait or misleading headlines to be fraudulent news unless they intentionally present obvious false information as true (Pen America, 2017).

The European Association for Viewers Interest (EAVI), an international nonprofit organization whose objective is to promote and empower citizens to be media literate users and consumers, identifies 10 types of misleading news: propaganda, clickbait, sponsored content, satire and hoax, error, partisan, conspiracy theory, pseudoscience, misinformation, and bogus. Each category is assigned a motivation to mislead such as money, power, humor, misinformation and passion, as well as a level of impact from neutral to high. EAVI recommends using the Center for Media Literacy's Five Core Concepts to analyze and evaluate the different types of misleading news (European Association for Viewers Interest, 2017).

These typologies provide insight into how to think about and define "fake news" in the changing news and information environment. The proliferation of untruths and fabricated news makes it ever more critical to learn how to spot false and misleading information, identify trustworthy news sources, and understand how the role of a free press affects our participation in a democracy.

Ask the Right Questions: Purpose

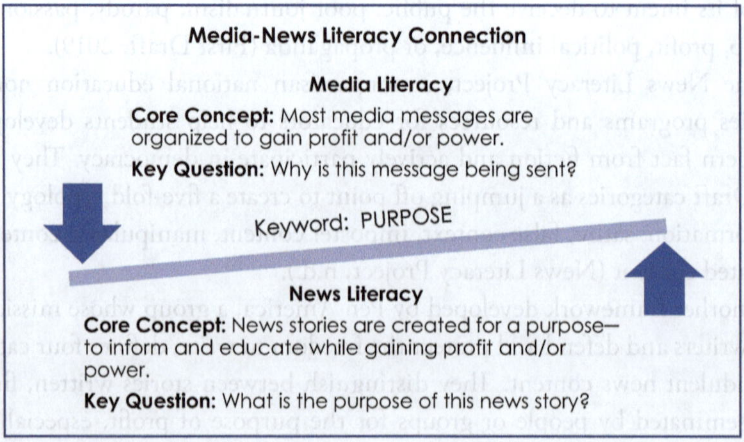

Fig. 3.4: Keyword — Purpose
Source: Author

Key Takeaways

1. The primary purpose of news is to establish truth and inform citizens about what is happening in the world.
2. The First Amendment of the U.S. Constitution empowers the press to function as the Fourth Estate — an unofficial branch of government that serves as a watchdog to monitor the legislative, judicial and executive branches for abuses of power.
3. Journalism is the only media practice protected by the U.S. Constitution because its role is to safeguard the public's access to reliable and trustworthy information so that they can responsibly participate in democracy.
4. Journalists are subject to a transparent news-gathering process that is verifiable, independent of conflicts of interest, and accountable to the public.
5. The practice of journalism is grounded in ethical codes of conduct and core principles of truthfulness, accuracy, independence, objectivity, impartiality, fairness, public accountability, and minimizing harm to sources, the issue in question, colleagues, and the public.
6. News is different from other types of information in its purpose, techniques, and outcome — news informs, opinion offers a point of view,

entertainment amuses and diverts, publicity promotes, advertising sells, propaganda manipulates and builds mass support, and raw, unfiltered user-generated content is a form of self-expression.

7. The Fifth Estate is an alternative to mainstream media created by the Internet and empowered by social networks where bloggers, citizen journalists, activists, social media influencers, and members of self-organizing communities can get their voices heard.
8. "Fake news" has a long history in American journalism and is widely used as a buzzword for misinformation and disinformation. The term also has been appropriated by politicians and other powerful people to characterize real news that is critical of them.
9. The difference between misinformation and disinformation is intent. Misinformation is not intentional rather an error in reporting that is corrected by the journalist or news organization or when a person unknowingly shares false information with no harm intended. Disinformation is the intentional spread of false and misleading information such as conspiracy theories, pseudoscience, false attribution, deepfakes, imposter or doctored content.
10. Malinformation intentionally inflicts harm by publishing private information without the person's permission or changing the context, date, time or place of actual content.

Guiding Questions

- Why was this story created, published and/or shared? Is the purpose to inform, change our mind, make us laugh, sell a product, promote an event or person for power or money?
- How do we know a media item is news? If it isn't news, is it an opinion, advertisement, publicity, entertainment, or someone's online self-expression? If it is expressed as a blog, tweet, meme, GIF or other format, why was it constructed this way?
- Is the media item a type of misinformation, disinformation or malinformation? Did the creator make a mistake, or are they intentionally trying to deceive and spread falsehoods for profit and/or political power, or take revenge on someone? Who benefits from this message? How do you know?
- Is the information part of the Fourth Estate or Fifth Estate? How might this affect the way a story is communicated and the reliability of the information?

Reflect: In what ways might partisanship or economic decisions affect the reporting of a news story? How does disinformation impact the democratic process? How does mis/dis/malinformation affect you?

References

Adams Family Papers. (1769, September). *1769 Septr 3D. Sunday.* John Adams diary 15, 30 January 1768, 10 August 1769 – 22 August 1770 [electronic edition]. *Adams Family Papers: An Electronic Archive.* Massachusetts Historical Society. https://www.masshist.org/digitaladams/archive/

Associated Press. (n.d.). *The Associated Press statement of news values and principles.* https://www.ap.org/about/news-values-and-principles/downloads/ap-news-values-and-principles.pdf

Associated Press. (2017, November 2). 'Fake news' is Collins Dictionary's word of the year 2017. https://apnews.com/article/47466c5e260149b1a23641b9e319fda6

Cambridge Dictionary. (n.d.). Fake news. https://dictionary.cambridge.org/us/dictionary/english/fake-news

Collins Dictionary. (2017, November 2). Word of the year shortlist. *Language Lovers Blog.* https://blog.collinsdictionary.com/language-lovers/collins-2017-word-of-the-year-shortlist/

Collins Dictionary. (n.d.). "Fake news." https://www.collinsdictionary.com/us/dictionary/english/fake-news

Dictionary.com. (n.d.). Fake news. https://www.dictionary.com/browse/fake-news

Digital Resource Center. (n.d.). V.I.A. Center for News Literacy, Stony Brook University. https://digitalresource.center/content/via

Dutton, W. (2009, February 14). The Fifth Estate emerging through the network of networks. *Prometheus, 27*(1), 1–15. https://doi.org/10.1080/08109020802657453

Edelson, L., Nguyen, M., Goldstein, I., Goga, O., Lauinger, T., & McCoy, D. (2021, March 3). *Far-right news sources on Facebook more engaging.* Cybersecurity for Democracy, Center for Cyber Security, New York University. https://medium.com/cybersecurity-for-democracy/far-right-news-sources-on-facebook-more-engaging-e04a01efae90

European Association for Viewers Interest. (2017). *Beyond 'fake news:' 10 types of misleading news.* https://eavi.eu/beyond-fake-news-10-types-misleading-info/

First Draft. (2019). *First Draft's essential guide to understanding information disorder.* https://firstdraftnews.org/long-form-article/understanding-information-disorder/

Freedom Forum. (2022, June). *2022 Update: First Amendment sparks and could bridge divide.* https://survey.freedomforum.org/2022-update/

Freedom Forum. (2021, September). *The First Amendment: Where America stands.* https://survey.freedomforum.org/content/uploads/2021/09/Freedom-Forum-Downloadable-Report.pdf

Garber, M. (2016, December 23). The scare quote: 2016 in a punctuation mark. *The Atlantic.* https://www.theatlantic.com/entertainment/archive/2016/12/the-scare-quote-2016-in-a-punctuation-mark/511319/

Goldstein, A. (2021, January 27). *Social media engagement with deceptive sites reached record highs in 2020.* [Blog Post]. The German Marshall Fund of the United States. https://www.gmfus.org/blog/2021/01/27/social-media-engagement-deceptive-sites-reached-record-highs-2020?utm_source=email&utm_medium=email&utm_campaign=press%20releases

Knight Foundation. (2018, January 16). *American views: Trust, media and democracy.* https://knightfoundation.org/wp-content/uploads/2019/06/KnightFoundation_AmericansViews_Client_Report_010917_Final_Updated.pdf

Kovach, B., & Rosenstiel, T. (2021). *The elements of journalism* (4th ed.). Crown.

McQueen, S. (2018). From yellow journalism to tabloids to clickbait: The origins of fake news in the United States. In D. Agosto (Ed.), *Information literacy and libraries in the age of fake news* (chapter 2, pp. 12–35). Libraries Unlimited.

Merriam-Webster. (n.d.). *The real story of 'fake news.'* https://www.merriam-webster.com/words-at-play/the-real-story-of-fake-news

News Literacy Project. (n.d). *Five types of misinformation.* [Infograhic]. https://newslit.org/wp-content/uploads/2021/11/Misinformation_Nov2021.pdf

NewseumED. (2019). *Fake news.* Fake News Exhibit. Washington, D.C.

Oxford English Dictionary. (n.d.). "Fake news." https://www-oed-com.libproxy.csun.edu/view/Entry/67776?redirectedFrom=fake+news#eid1264306660

Oxford English Dictionary. [@OED]. (2019, October 9). *A notable entry in the October update to the OED is the term 'fake news.'* [Tweet]. Twitter. https://twitter.com/OED/status/1181991604170694658

Parkinson, R. (2016, November 25). Fake news? That's a very old story. *Washington Post.* https://www.washingtonpost.com/opinions/fake-news-thats-a-very-old-story/2016/11/25/c8b1f3d4-b330-11e6-8616-52b15787add0_story.html

Pen America. (2017, October 12). *Faking news: Fraudulent news and the fight for truth.* https://pen.org/wp-content/uploads/2017/11/2017-Faking-News-11.2.pdf

Pew Research Center. (2016, December 15). *Many Americans believe "fake news" is sowing confusion.* https://www.journalism.org/wp-content/uploads/sites/8/2016/12/PJ_2016.12.15_fake-news_FINAL.pdf

Radio Television Digital News Association. (2015). *RTDNA code of ethics.* https://www.rtdna.org/content/rtdna_code_of_ethics

Society of Professional Journalists. (2014). *SPJ code of ethics.* https://www.spj.org/ethicscode.asp

Tandoc, E., Lim, Z., & Ling, R. (2017). Defining "fake news:" A typology of scholarly definitions. *Digital Journalism 6*(2), 137–153. https://doi.org/10.1080/21670811.2017.1360143

Wardle, C., & Derakhshan, H. (2018). Thinking about 'information disorder': Formats of misinformation, disinformation and mal-information. In C. Ireton & J. Posetti (Eds.), *Journalism, 'Fake News' and Disinformation: A Handbook for Journalism Education and Training* (module 2, pp. 44–56). United Nations Educational, Scientific and Cultural Organization. https://en.unesco.org/fightfakenews

4

Who Writes the News?

When you read, watch or listen to the news, have you ever considered who writes the story or who shot the photograph or filmed the video? Is it a reporter from a mainstream news outlet? A blogger? A news-writing bot? A celebrity's publicist? A social media influencer? Does it matter?

Who Is a Journalist?

Traditionally, news stories are written by trained professional journalists employed on the staff of news organizations. *A journalist is part of the process of gathering, writing, editing, and disseminating news at a news outlet — reporters, editors, correspondents, columnists, anchors, producers, photographers, videographers, and freelancers who are contracted by a news organization for a special assignment.* Journalists work for many different types of news media platforms — mainstream newspapers and magazines with print and online versions, radio and TV broadcast and cable news stations, digital-only news publications, newsletters, newsfeeds, news apps, and news agencies and syndicates that supply news and features to subscribing news outlets.

There is no one type of journalist. There are different types of journalists who use various journalistic writing forms. For example, a reporter is a specific type of journalist who writes straight news stories. Have you noticed that reporters at news organizations tend to cover the same topic area? Unless they are a *general assignment reporter* who covers a wide range of stories, journalists specialize in a particular area called a *news beat*. A news reporter's beat is a specific subject area, government agency, organization or institution. The reporter might cover politics, national news, international news, law enforcement, business and the economy, media and technology, science and environment, education, sports, religion, weather, health, fitness, food, entertainment, arts and culture, lifestyle and leisure. As new issues arise in society, new beats are created. With so much problematic online content, disinformation is now a beat at many news outlets.

What Are the Different Types of Journalism?

The main types of journalism involve news, opinion, investigative and feature writing. Each type of journalistic writing has its own technique and is used for a specific purpose. No matter what journalists write about, they all are obligated to comply with the same professional code of ethical conduct and transparent news-gathering process that is verifiable, independent and accountable. They verify the facts, disclose any financial or personal conflicts of interest, take responsibility for the reliability of their facts, and publicly correct any errors.

It is important to understand how these journalistic writing forms differ from one another, especially news and opinion. Distinguishing between factual and opinion content can be confusing for news consumers — especially online news and social media — and unduly influence how people might interpret information and understand an issue. If news consumers are politically aware and open-minded about an issue, opinion journalism can offer new insights, challenge assumptions, and help make an informed decision about an issue. To avoid confusion between fact-based news and opinion formats, some news organizations clearly label an opinion piece to differentiate it from news reports.

How is news different from opinion?

Straight news reports are fact-based stories about current local, national and international events that explain who, what, when, where, why and how — known as 5Ws and H — in the first sentence. News stories are accurate, balanced and fair, properly attributed and written in the third person. In newspapers, the most important news stories of the day appear in a prominent place which is the front page at the top. Political stories will be on the front page of the first section of a newspaper and inside that section, while business, sports and entertainment stories will be in their respective sections, unless the story is so important that it warrants front-page coverage in the first section of the newspaper. Or if the sports or entertainment story is about a huge business deal, then that angle of the story may be reported on the front page of the business section. For broadcast and cable news, the most important stories will be at the start of the newscast, and for websites and news apps, they will be featured at the top of the webpage.

Opinion writing is distinctly separate from news reports. Unlike fact-based news reporting that is required to remain neutral in order to give a balanced and fair treatment to the story, opinion writers express their personal viewpoints and base their opinions on facts. They may write in the first person, use sarcasm or hyperbole, or parody a person or subject. Opinion pieces usually appear on a page dedicated to them or are labeled as opinion.

Editorials, columns and reviews, are all opinion writing. Editorials are usually about a current event, issue, policy or politician and are found on the editorial page and the page opposite it called the op-ed page. Columnists and reviewers usually specialize in a subject area and their columns are located in that section. Sports commentary is in the sports section, business in the business section, TV, film, music, food and restaurant reviews in the entertainment or feature section, along with advice and celebrity news.

What is the difference between an editorial and an op-ed?

Editorials express the view of the news organization and are written by its editorial board, while *op-eds* are opinion editorials that express an opinion of a writer and is signed by the writer. Opinion writers either work for the news outlet and are hired to express their opinion in a column or are outside contributors not affiliated with the publication. The word op-ed comes from "opposite the editorial page," which is where op-eds traditionally appear along with letters-to-the-editor in a newspaper. The purpose of the op-ed page is to provide a public space where a diversity of voices can express thought-provoking opinion that stimulates discussion about an issue of public importance. Editorial cartoons that combine art and commentary about current events and are signed by the cartoonist also appear on these pages.

What is the difference between an op-ed and a guest essay?

An op-ed and a guest essay are essentially the same thing. Like an op-ed, a *guest essay* is a contributor opinion piece written by a person invited by the publication to express their view about a topic. In 2021, *The New York Times* changed the name from Op-Ed to Guest Essay. According to *The Times* opinion editor, who oversees the editorial board and the Opinion section, the change was made because the term "opposite the editorial page" is outdated in the digital media landscape where opinion pieces do not appear on the page opposite the newspaper's editorial as they do in print newspapers. The word Guest Essay was chosen because it better reflects the relationship between *The Times* and the invited opinion writer and the newspaper's mission to champion diverse voices and views (Kingsbury, 2021). The Guest Essay appears in the Opinion section and is clearly labeled with the title Guest Essay above the headline and the opinion writer's byline and one-line bio below the headline to identify that it is an opinion piece, who wrote it, and the person's credentials.

What is the difference between news analysis and opinion?

News analysis is different from opinion journalism in a very basic way: *opinion writing* promotes a particular point of view while *news analysis* provides context and interpretation of issues without taking sides.

What is investigative reporting?

Investigative journalism is the watchdog role of the press to uncover the truth and inform the public about misconduct, corruption and other wrongdoings in society. When politicians use their office for personal gain, or companies conceal unethical practices, or police cover up procedural violations, it is journalists who have the responsibility to gather the evidence and provide a context for the public to understand. *Investigative stories* involve in-depth reporting and original research that uses data and documents to ascertain public accountability and attain social justice.

What is a feature story?

We've all read stories about celebrity breakups and makeups, or how to shed those five extra pounds, or the latest trends in tech accessories. These are not about breaking news or even necessarily related to current events. *Feature stories* are about people, trends, or any issues that appeal to us because of the topic, story angle or writing style.

If a Journalist Didn't Write This, Then Who Did?

It has been said that journalists write the "first rough draft of history." There is debate about who said this first, but many attribute it to Philip Graham, former publisher and owner of *The Washington Post* (Shafer, 2010): "Let us today drudge on about our inescapably impossible task of providing every week a first rough draft of history that will never be completed about a world we can never really understand" (as cited in Katharine Graham, 1997, p. 324).

With the proliferation of news and information on the Internet, no longer are newspapers always considered the first permanent record of an event. Instead, digital and social media, overrun with inaccuracies, rumors, conspiracy theories and other "fake news," have become the first rough draft of history, and good journalism is the second draft responsible for investigating the underlying truth of the first draft and retelling the story (Harkin, 2019). This paradigm shift profoundly affects us all because whoever writes the stories has the power to tell our shared history and shape our worldview.

Who is contributing to this Internet-driven rough first draft of history? Anyone who contributes stories and commentary to the Fifth Estate — bloggers, citizen journalists, proclaimed experts, social media influencers, lobbyists, activists, conspiracy theorists, as well as bots and chatbots whose content can be inaccurate, biased or entirely fabricated. Even news consumers generate stories when they like, post comments, tweet and retweet. Does it matter who writes the story? Of course it matters because facts matter and not just anyone is a journalist.

Why does it matter that a journalist writes the story?

Simply put, journalists are media professionals trained in their craft, follow ethical principles of their profession, and are transparent about the news-gathering process. Non-journalists are not part of news organizations and do not have to follow the same standards and practices as journalists, which means they can publish without regard to the authenticity or reliability of the information. They may contribute, unintentionally or intentionally, to the spread of disinformation. Before reading a news story, or tuning into a newscast, or clicking on a link, check the source — where it appears, who created it, and who pays for the content. Also be aware of pseudo-journalists and others who can be confused with journalists.

Who is a pseudo-journalist?

Pseudo-journalists look like news reporters and news anchors and work for news organizations, but they are not. They present themselves as journalists but act more like pundits who do not adhere to journalism's professional code of ethics and are not committed to conventional standards of conduct. They sound like opinion journalists but use news formats to pursue an agenda that typically promotes a false narrative based on logical fallacies, often discrediting legitimate journalists, and package the analysis in sound bites that are easy to share — other reporters, pundits and bloggers frequently repeat what they say to their audiences. Some are *opinion hosts* on major networks who mix opinion with news, commentary and analysis in a hybrid format disguised as a news show. When audiences cannot discern the difference between opinion and news, it can contribute to the spread of falsehoods, mislead the public, and threaten democracy.

Is a pundit a journalist?

Pundits are not journalists. They are "talking heads" who are contracted by a news organization to share their opinion or commentary on a particular topic about which they are supposedly very knowledgeable or a known expert in their field. While we are probably most familiar with political pundits, some of whom are aligned with political parties or candidates, even paid spokespersons, pundits can be an expert on any topic, from finance and the economy, to international relations and criminal justice, to health, technology, sports, entertainment, the arts and fashion. Some are former public officials, political advisers, policy analysts or military officers, while others are healthcare providers, business professionals, university researchers and scholars, or representatives from think tanks or advocacy groups.

Typically, pundits appear on a panel with a mix of journalists and non-journalists and play a key role in disseminating ideas about an issue currently in the news. This hybrid-news commentary format makes it hard to differentiate the moderator from the pundits and the journalists and blurs the line between news and opinion. Unlike opinion journalists who are grounded in professional codes of ethics and obligated to base their opinion on verifiable facts, disclose conflicts of interest and correct themselves if they misspeak, pundits can say whatever they like and are not held accountable, even if they intentionally misinform the audience to sway their opinion about an issue.

Is a "citizen journalist" a journalist?

If we happen to be at the scene of an accident, shoot a video and post it online, does that make us a journalist? Or if we send the video or photos to a news outlet or write an eyewitness account and they use it, or present an unreported angle of a story and they report it, or contribute a news tip, story idea or blog post, are we a journalist? In a literal sense, we are a journalist but not a professional journalist, rather a citizen journalist. A *citizen journalist* is a public citizen who may play an active role in news gathering but is not trained as a reporter and is not employed by a news organization. In certain instances, a reporter or news outlet might track down a person whose photos or footage they saw on social media to use in their reporting of the story.

Anyone can be a citizen journalist, especially if they have a smartphone or other way to document or discuss their experience or views about an event. Citizen journalists are individual content creators who have disrupted the news-gathering process. They do not have to cite source material or quote sources, their reporting tends to reflect their individual experiences and concerns, and they publish across social media platforms. With no professional ties to news organizations, their goals and motivations are not the same as journalists. Some are motivated by self-serving interests such as enhancing their status or expressing their creativity, while others want to serve the public interest.

Researchers have identified four types of citizen journalists based on their form of contribution and editorial control: (1) *participatory citizen journalists* contribute news, opinion and information to traditional news outlets, often first-hand accounts and visual content of breaking news that journalists are unable to access; (2) *para citizen journalists* raise awareness about an event that is happening live by contributing news, opinion and information to a collaborative news stream that monitors the event to help the community make sense of it and provide emergency instructions if needed; (3) *news media watchdog citizen journalists* verify the accuracy of a story, interpret and critique news performance, and provide in-depth news analysis about public affairs; and (4) *community citizen journalists* report local events and issues not covered by journalists and maintain complete gatekeeping and editorial control over content from news-gathering to publication (Miller, 2019).

No matter which type of citizen journalist a person is, they contribute a distinct perspective to the narrative of a news story. Sometimes the person is in the right place at the right time to capture a moment of history that can shape the nation. That was the case of the first noteworthy citizen journalists who filmed the exact moment President John F. Kennedy was assassinated in 1963 and who recorded the police beating of Rodney King that led to the 1992 L.A. riots. These were accidents of fate that demonstrate the potential power of citizen journalism.

Who was the first citizen journalist?

For years, the first citizen journalist was thought to be George Holliday who caught on camera the violent police attack of Rodney King on March 31, 1991. After leading police on a nearly 8-mile car chase through the streets of Los Angeles for a traffic violation, Rodney King was pulled from his car and brutally beaten by police. Holliday lived across the street from where the police stopped King, heard sirens and helicopters circling overhead, and grabbed his new camcorder to record whatever was happening. Standing less than 100 feet away on his apartment balcony, he was not expecting to see police kicking and tasering a man on the ground. Not knowing if it had any news value, he brought the tape to local news station KTLA and they broadcast it that night. If Holliday had not been there at that moment, this violent attack would not have been recorded and reported. It would not have led to the arrest of four police officers and their acquittal on state criminal charges that sparked the 1992 Los Angeles riots (Abramovitch, 2021).

Years before, Abraham Zapruder was filming President John F. Kennedy's motorcade in downtown Dallas when he unexpectedly captured the assassination of the president on November 22, 1963. Zapruder loved to make home movies with his 8mm camera and was there to record the president's visit to share with his family. Shaken and confused after the fatal shooting, Zapruder headed back to his office when a *Dallas Morning News* reporter, who had been standing next to him watching the motorcade, approached him about the film. Zapruder did not want the film to be sensationalized and agreed to hand over a copy to the Secret Service on condition it be used to help with the government investigation. Shortly after, he entrusted the rights to the original film to *Life Magazine,* but a bootleg copy eventually made its way to Geraldo Rivera who broadcast it on national television in 1975. Until that time, the 26 seconds of film, which shows the assassination from beginning to end in color but without sound, was withheld from public view. Secrecy around this film led to a number of conspiracy theories about the assassination that continue to circulate today (Rosenbaum, 2013). Not until much later was Zapruder recognized as the first notable citizen journalist. In 1999, the Zapruder family donated the film, photographs, and copyright to the Sixth Floor Museum in Dallas where it is preserved as a national archive.

What is crowdsourced journalism?

Crowdsourcing is another type of online citizen participation in journalism. Journalists and media organizations use crowdsourcing to gather information for a story, or establish the credibility of information or a source, or identify misinformation or disinformation circulating online. For example, journalists might send out a request on social media to individuals who live in the area of a natural disaster to share their personal experiences and eyewitness accounts. Or they might fact-check the credibility of a photograph they accessed online by contacting a group of people who are familiar with the location and event captured in the image. While crowdsourcing engages citizen participants and contributes to the watchdog role of journalism, it can compromise journalistic standards of objectivity, fairness and accuracy if journalists are not transparent about how they selected the individuals or groups and consider potential participant bias (Aitamurto, 2019).

Crowdsourced journalism also may be a potentially viable strategy to help combat mis/disinformation. The approach is to ask a crowdsourced community to rate the trustworthiness of news sites and then apply those trust ratings to configure algorithms to display more content from trustworthy sources and less from untrustworthy ones in the social media platform newsfeed (Pennycock & Rand, 2019).

Are blogs and tweets considered journalism?

The short answer is, it depends. It depends on who is writing the blog or tweet. And it depends on whether it is well researched and fact-based or someone's opinion that might or might not be based on facts.

In the Blogosphere and Twittersphere, anyone can create and publish content. Many bloggers are experts in their fields and share their knowledge by blogging, while others know little about a topic and are simply sharing their opinion they may or may not have verified, or are passing on information that may not be accurate, even made up or a hoax or conspiracy theory. Still others are professional journalists who "live blog" or "live tweet" updates to breaking news stories as information becomes available. Or they may be journalists who use social media to write news analysis or commentary that expands on news stories they published in their news outlet. Blogs and tweets offer journalists ways to connect with audiences in a more informal and conversational style.

The savvy news consumer who gets news from blog posts and tweets needs to know how to differentiate between facts and opinion and how to distinguish between credible and fraudulent information on those networking sites. Check the source, verify the facts, regardless of whether it is a news report or opinion piece, and think critically about who the author is and who is paying for the content.

Ask the Right Questions: Authorship

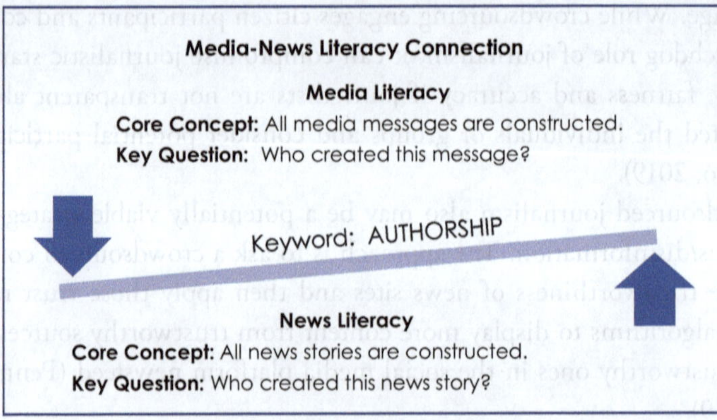

Fig. 4.1: Keyword — Authorship
Source: Author

Key Takeaways

1. News is constructed by trained professional journalists employed on the staffs of news organizations — reporters, correspondents, anchors, editors, columnists, producers, photographers, videographers, freelancers, and others who gather, write, edit and disseminate news for a news outlet.
2. There are different types of journalists who use different writing forms — general assignment reporters, beat reporters, investigative, feature and opinion writers.

3. Pseudo-journalists present themselves as journalists employed by news organizations but do not adhere to journalism's professional code of ethics and standards of conduct. Instead they use news formats to pursue an agenda that typically promotes a false narrative, often discredits legitimate journalists, misleads their audience, and threatens democracy.
4. Pundits are not journalists but often are confused with them because they share their opinions on news programs and play a key role in disseminating ideas about current events. Unlike journalists, pundits can say whatever they like without being held accountable, even if they intentionally misinform the public or try to influence their view.
5. Different types of non-journalists publish or publicize stories online — citizen journalists present unreported angles of a story, bloggers and proclaimed experts offer their verified and unverified knowledge about a topic, activists, lobbyists and special interest groups promote a cause, advertisers and social media influencers market their products, and news consumers generate stories when they like, comment, tweet and retweet.
6. The difference between journalists and non-journalists is that journalists are employed by a news organization, trained in the craft of journalism, grounded in professional codes of ethics, obligated to verify the facts, disclose any personal or financial conflicts of interest, and take responsibility to publicly correct any errors in their reporting.
7. Crowdsourcing is a type of online citizen participation in journalism in which journalists and media organizations enlist a large number of social media users for a task, such as providing eyewitness accounts of a disaster, establishing the credibility of a source, or identifying mis/disinformation circulating online.
8. Traditionally, news has been called "the first rough draft of history," but recently social media — despite being overrun with disinformation — is displacing news as the first rough draft, making quality journalism the second rough draft of history responsible for fact-checking social media and retelling the story.

Guiding Questions

- Who created the news story? Check who wrote, photographed, edited, produced, and distributed it. Did a professional journalist? If a journalist did not write or share the story, then who did? Or did you generate the story and why?

- What type of journalist wrote the news item? Is it written by a general assignment or beat reporter, or an opinion, investigative or feature writer? How do you know? If it is an opinion, who wrote it? Consider the difference between an opinion writer, editorial board, guest essayist, and reviewer.
- Are pseudo-journalists, pundits, bloggers, and citizen journalists considered journalists? In what ways are they similar or different from a journalist?
- How do creators of blogs, tweets, memes, press releases and video news releases affect the news process? What do special interest groups, government officials, lobbyists, advertisers, social media influencers, and news-writing bots have to do with journalism?
- Where did the news item originate? Was it from a professional news organization, alternative news source or social media platform? How was it shared?

Reflect: How do you know who is responsible for the news story and when and where it originally appeared? Why does it matter that a journalist writes the story?

References

Abramovitch, S. (2021, March 3). Flashback: How a plumber altered history by taping the attack on Rodney King. *Hollywood Reporter.* https://www.hollywoodreporter.com/lifestyle/lifestyle-news/flashback-how-a-plumber-altered-history-by-taping-the-attack-on-rodney-king-4141644/

Aitamurto, T. (2019). Crowdsourcing in journalism. *Oxford Research Encyclopedia of Communication.* https://doi.org/10.1093/acrefore/9780190228613.013.795

Graham, K. (1997). *Personal history.* A.A. Knopf.

Harkin, J. (2019, January 14). Journalism is now the second draft of history. *Columbia Journalism Review.* https://www.cjr.org/opinion/journalism-is-now-the-second-draft-of-history.php

Kingsbury, K. (2021, April 27). Why we're retiring the term 'op-ed.' *The New York Times,* p. A22. https://www.nytimes.com/2021/04/26/opinion/nyt-opinion-oped-redesign.html

Miller, S. (2019). Citizen journalism. *Oxford Research Encyclopedia of Communication.* https://doi.org/10.1093/acrefore/9780190228613.013.786

Pennycock, G., & Rand, D. (2019). Fighting misinformation on social media using crowdsourced judgments of news source quality. *Proceedings of the National Academy of Science.* https://doi.org/10.1073/pnas.1806781116

Rosenbaum, R. (2013, October). What does the Zapruder film really mean? *Smithsonian Magazine.* https://www.smithsonianmag.com/history/what-does-the-zapruder-film-really-tell-us-14194/

Shafer, J. (2010, August 30). Who said it first? *Slate*. https://slate.com/news-and-politics/2010/08/on-the-trail-of-the-question-who-first-said-or-wrote-that-journalism-is-the-first-rough-draft-of-history.html

5

What Makes This Story Newsworthy?

With billions of events happening simultaneously in the world, what makes one news and another not? Put simply, news is the account of the event and not the event itself. For a story to be news, there has to be a report about it in a news outlet. Why are some stories selected over others? Who determines the newsworthiness of a story? Which storytelling techniques make a story more newsworthy? What types of stories attract audience interest?

Who Decides What Is News?

Who decides what is newsworthy is a function of the journalism *gatekeeping process*. With so many events happening in the world, the role of gatekeepers is to filter information and select stories they think are important and will resonate with their audience. Traditionally, gatekeepers are editors at newspapers and news magazines, news directors and producers at broadcast and cable stations, social media editors at Internet outlets and social networking platforms, and others with the responsibility to filter news and information to disseminate to the public. Journalists themselves are gatekeepers because they decide the story angle and what information to include in their reporting of the story.

Which stories are selected as newsworthy and how the stories are framed — what facts are emphasized and deemphasized, who is quoted, which visuals or sound bites are used, and where the story is placed in the publication, broadcast or online — tell readers, viewers and listeners what is important and affects their understanding of the issue, event or person the story is about. This is the *agenda-setting effect* of news.

Agenda setting focuses public attention on certain issues and not others. Gatekeepers' story selection and storytelling gives them the ability to tell us *what to think about* and, depending how the story is framed, *how to think about it.* This is a powerful effect because it can shape our social reality and worldview, influence our attitudes and opinions, and govern our actions. When we recognize what determines newsworthiness, we begin to understand what might influence our perceptions, as well as other people's perceptions, of what is and what is not important in our community, our country, and throughout the world.

What Determines the Newsworthiness of a Story?

While the emergent digital media ecosystem is transforming how news is delivered, what makes a story newsworthy is not changing — the same editorial decisions and news values apply to print, broadcast, digital and online media. There are three main factors that determine newsworthiness: *a story's news values, the news organization's editorial judgment,* and *audience interest.*

What are news values?

News values are the elements of a story that determine whether the issue or event is worth covering, how relevant it is to the audience, and how prominent the coverage will be in the news outlet. While news values can be specific to a culture, there are several that are considered universal that drive newsworthiness (Digital Resource Center, n.d.): the *prominence* of the newsmaker, that is, the person who the story is about, the *timeliness, importance, and magnitude* of the event, its *relevance and proximity* to people, whether the story is of *human interest* or about *conflict or change* or something *unusual or odd* that happened. The more news values that drive a story, the more prominent the coverage it will receive in the news outlet.

What Makes a Story Newsworthy?

Which events get reported depends on the news value of the story as determined by the editors and journalists. The more news values a story contains, the bigger the story and the more likely the story goes viral. There are 10 universal news values that drive a story's newsworthiness.

Timeliness. How current is the event? Is it breaking news? Does it commemorate an occasion or the anniversary of an event?

Proximity. How nearby or close to home is the event? Is it local, national or international news that affects the community, the country or the world?

Human Interest. How relatable or inspirational is the story? Can we empathize or identify with the people or circumstances? Does it make us sad or depressed, angry or outraged, happy or overjoyed?

Conflict. Is the story about a controversy or confrontation between individuals, groups, institutions or ideas? Is it about a political power struggle, sports rivalry, or conflict that reflects a local, national or international problem?

Change. How do scientific discoveries, policy changes or attitude shifts affect individuals?

Importance. How important is the event to the community, the country or the world? What are the social, political, economic or cultural implications?

Magnitude. Is the story driven by numbers? How does it compare with or predict similar events?

Relevance. Does the story matter to the audience? How does it affect decisions we need to make in our lives? How far-reaching is the story's impact on the audience?

Prominence. Is the story about a prominent person, public figure, celebrity or athlete? Is the newsmaker someone well-known for their accomplishments?

Unusualness. Is the event out-of-the-ordinary, strange, shocking or sensational? Is it a bizarre or rare occurrence such as "man bites dog" and not "dog bites man"?

As new media technology emerges enabling new and innovative news formats to evolve, traditional news values may not apply as well. The 24/7 news cycle and push notifications have transformed our sense of timeliness and immediacy. The interconnectedness of the world has redefined proximity for certain issues and events. The spread of disinformation has made news outlets a vehicle for emboldening conflict as well as reporting about it. Covering change has become a big story that affects us all as we continuously adapt to a new normal for the way we work, play, communicate and interact.

Our values are changing along with our news habits and content choices. News consumers are sharing, curating and customizing their news. Journalists and journalism scholars are re-examining news criteria to reflect the emergent digital news media ecosystem and changing news behaviors. News values that tap inclusion, authenticity, verification, accountability, accessibility, personalization, shareability and clickability are some that could potentially reach more diverse and younger news consumers (Clark, 2016; Mast & Temmerman, 2021).

What drives editorial judgment?

News editors and producers make editorial judgments about which stories are newsworthy. Their judgments are driven by news values and other factors: *compelling content, a scoop or exclusive story,* and *audience interest*. What is considered newsworthy are visual stories with powerful images or video. Stories driven by conflict and human interest that engage the audience. A scoop that a journalist from the news outlet is the first to report the story and beats out the competition. An exclusive story or interview a journalist is offered and no other news outlet has the story. A story that the audience would want to read, and even share, because of their interests.

Editorial judgment also determines which stories in the news that day will receive more attention and what kind of attention. More newsworthy stories will be more prominently placed, use visual and audio techniques to underscore the importance of a story and focus audience attention on the story, and take up more news space — number of minutes or column inches devoted to the story as well as the number of days the story is in the news.

Essentially, the more *newsworthy* a story is determined to be, the more importance it is given by a news outlet and, in turn, the more attention it is likely to receive from the audience. Creative techniques signal a story's significance to attract audience attention — catchy and large, bold headlines, photographs, charts, pull-quotes, boxes, use of color, prominent story placement on the front page above the fold in print newspapers and above the scroll in online versions, and multimedia elements in digital editions embedded in the main story or positioned alongside the story text.

Broadcast and cable news feature the more newsworthy stories at the start of the newscast and use compelling graphics, interviews, eyewitness accounts, original footage or audio recording, live breaking news, and teasers before a commercial break to indicate the importance of a story. Newsworthiness on social media is visible in the numbers of clicks, likes, shares, reposts, retweets, hashtags, a news story going viral, or its re-presentation as memes and GIFs that get a lot of notice. To capture audience attention, news organizations also produce stories in different formats and disseminate them across media platforms, including news aggregator websites where users can view news and updates from a variety of sources.

How does the audience affect what is newsworthy?

The newsworthiness of a story is also based on audience demand for information that is happening now and affects their lives. Editorial decisions weigh what the audience wants versus what the audience needs to be informed. Stories that capture audience interest are more newsworthy. A story about legislative tax reform may be more important than a story about a celebrity's medical diagnosis. However, if the audience finds the celebrity story more interesting, then that story might end up as or more prominently featured. To better serve audiences, news organizations use surveys, polls and other types of audience data to drive news judgment, including clicks, views, likes and shares in online editions and on social media platforms.

How Is a News Story Constructed?

When we think about the news, the first thing that probably comes to mind is a TV news broadcast. Or a print newspaper. Or an online version of the print newspaper. Or a radio news program. Or a podcast. Or a newsfeed on a social media platform. These are simply different means of conveyance. Each one uses creative techniques specific to the media technology and platform to construct the news story and distribute it.

The choice of media platform to construct and distribute the news story limits or broadens the scope of the story. Take newspapers as an example. Traditional print newspapers use several basic news elements that include a text narrative to tell the story, headlines, photographs, graphics, sidebars and pullout quotes, while online versions use the same basic elements enhanced with audio, video, animated graphics, GIFs, memes and other multimedia techniques that extend the story's reach on Twitter, Facebook, Instagram, TikTok, and other social media networks.

No matter which means of news production and transmission are used, journalists are grounded in the same basic reporting and writing principles to construct a news story, as well as trained in multimedia storytelling techniques for their respective news platform. Journalists follow consistent style guidelines for grammar, spelling, punctuation and language usage, and use the same basic elements of news storytelling: develop the story around a main point or focus, include a beginning, middle and end, answer the questions who, what, when, where, why and how, and explain the context with background information that provides a perspective to understand the story more fully.

What are the common story elements?

Like any profession, journalism has its own language to describe what journalists do and how they do it. Knowing basic journalism jargon is part of being news literate. Let's start with story elements. There are several common elements to every story: a beginning, middle and end, headline, dateline, byline, source attribution, and visuals such as a photo with a caption and credit.

Beginning: Lead

The first sentence of the story is called the *lead*. The lead is one of the most important parts of the story because it is the hook. The lead tells us what the story is about and either keeps us reading or makes us lose interest and move on. The type of lead depends on the type of story. For example, a straight news story starts summarizing the main points with who, what, when, where, why and how and elaborates on these points in the rest of the story, while a feature story begins with an anecdote or description of a person, place or event and then explains the story focus.

Lead or Lede?

An alternative spelling of the word lead is lede (both are pronounced "lēēd"). Lede replaced lead in newsrooms during the 1970s to avoid confusion with other uses of the word. Lead referred to the first sentence of the story as well as thin strips of metal used to separate type in Linotype printing presses. Even though this printing press is no longer used in newsrooms, some journalists prefer to use lede or use the spellings interchangeably (Clark, 2019).

Middle: More Facts

The *middle* is the body of the story that uses facts, information and quotes or sound bites to elaborate on the main focus, provide background and context, and explain how the news affects the community.

End: Story End

The *end* is exactly that: the end of the story because there is no more known information that pertains to the story's focus. The most common endings contain a statement or quote that summarizes the story or refers to future action. If the story is developing with more facts to come, then that is the end statement.

Headline

The *headline* identifies the story focus and appears at the top of the news article. Some headlines have subheads or secondary headlines to give the reader more insight into what the story is about. Headlines are important because they can either grab our attention and persuade us to read the first sentence or not draw us in and dismiss the story altogether.

Dateline

The *dateline* identifies where the story was filed, usually a city, and appears at the start of the first paragraph. If the story originates from a news agency that provides syndicated news to the news organization for a fee, then the dateline will be the name of the news agency. For example, if the story comes from Associated Press, abbreviated AP, then the dateline will be AP.

Byline

A *byline* identifies the reporter who wrote the story. The byline usually appears under the headline with the word "by" and the name of the journalist. If more than one reporter wrote the story, all names are listed. If other reporters contributed to the story but did not write it, those names are usually at the end of the story. There is a trend not to include bylines on the online version of the newspaper's front page and instead place them on the page where the article lives after clicking on the headline. For news broadcasts, reporters state their names at the start and/or end of the story. If a reporter's name is not given, check the credibility of the source.

Nut Graf

A *nut graf* is a paragraph that explains the essence of the story — "nut" stands for nutshell and "graf" is short for paragraph — it's the kernel of the story summarized in a paragraph. A story sometimes has more than one nut graf. Nut grafs are usually used in feature stories to connect the lead to the details of the story and provide context to help readers understand why the story is important.

Photo Caption and Credit

A *caption* is the line below the photo that describes what or who is in the photo, and a *credit* identifies the photojournalist who shot the photo or the media company that supplied the photo. Another word for caption is cutline.

Source Attribution

As part of the news-gathering process, journalists bring together facts, quotes and opinions from the best available sources and attribute this information to them in their story. *Source attribution* is the phrase in the news story that identifies the name and title of the person interviewed or the publication, public record or document where the information comes from in the news report. These sources are referred to as *on the record* because they allow themselves to be quoted and publicly identified. The story will state something like: *"According to (name and title of person)"* or *"According to a recent poll conducted by (name of agency or institution)"* or *"(person's name and title) said."* In some instances, journalists use information from a source who does not want to be identified and provides the information anonymously or off the record.

Anonymous Sources

Anonymous sources are non-attributable and off the record. In these circumstances, the source provides information to a journalist but for certain reasons will not go on record to be publicly named and/or identify where the information came from. It may be because the information is allowed to be made public, but the source is not authorized to speak publicly. Or the source may allow their name to be used for some information but not for other more sensitive information. Or the source may need to protect their identity and use an alias because of domestic violence, substance abuse or classified information. If the source is anonymous, look for wording that describes the person's position such as: *"A spokesperson for…"* or *"A government official briefed on the situation…"* or *"A player on the team…"* or *"People familiar with the investigation…"*

Levels of Source Attribution
Before an interview, reporters and their sources agree on what information can and cannot be directly quoted. Rules for attribution are established by the news organization based on general guidelines.
On the record: The source allows their name to be publicly identified and their words directly quoted.
On background or *not for attribution:* The source is not publicly identified by name but allows the information to be quoted or paraphrased and their position to be described in general terms.
Off the record: The information the source provides is not for publication but the reporter can use it to better understand an issue and get other sources to confirm it on the record or on background.

Why do journalists use information from anonymous sources?

Among the biggest misunderstandings about journalism is anonymous sources. Most news consumers think that an anonymous source is not known to a journalist or to the public. This is only half true. Anonymous sources are known to journalists but not to news consumers. While journalists strive to identify sources who are on the record, at times they may rely on an anonymous source who is credible if they could not otherwise get the information and it is vital to the story. Information journalists use from anonymous sources is based on the source's knowledge directly related to the story and not on opinion, confirmed by multiple sources with first-hand knowledge, and approved and vetted by the managing editor. Journalists also consider an anonymous source's bias and motivation for sharing the information, and they are obligated not to disclose the source's identity. When anonymous sourcing is a document and not an interview, then journalists explain how the document was obtained.

What Are Journalism Story Techniques?

Journalists use different techniques to construct news stories. While all news stories answer the 5Ws and H — who, what, when, where, why and how — the order in which they are told depends on the type of story, journalism writing form, and media platform. Here are some common journalism storytelling techniques:

- *Inverted pyramid:* Straight news stories that are usually written with the most important facts first — 5Ws and H — followed by information in descending order of importance
- *Wall Street Journal or circle technique:* Feature stories that show how ordinary people are affected by trends, issues or events that begin with an anecdote or quote to illustrate the main focus, then detail point by point what the story is about and why it is important, and circle back to the beginning with a closing anecdote or quote
- *Hourglass or martini glass structure:* Crime, disaster and other dramatic news stories that are best told by starting with the most important facts, then shift to a chronological step-by-step account of how the events unfolded, and end with a memorable quote or surprise twist
- *List technique:* Soft news that lends itself to bulleting key points to help readers quickly scan the text in stories about research findings or meeting actions, or features about people or programs, or press releases by public relations specialists
- *Question and answer:* Commonly used for personality profiles and to explain complex issues, policies and programs
- *Sections:* In-depth investigative and lengthy feature stories divide the story into sections separated by a line, large capital letter or other graphic device to make it easier for readers to follow, especially on smartphones and tablets where they can click to the next section
- *Explainers:* Explains in detail the "how" and "why" something happened and background and context for "who," "what" and "where" using a conversational tone with simple words and sentences to answer questions that an ordinary person might ask or want to know about a complex issue that impacts their lives

Inverted Pyramid Style: 5Ws and H

The *inverted pyramid style* is the most common story structure for hard news. This reporting style tells the story in an upside-down way using the 5Ws and H — who, what, when, where, why and how — in the first sentence to summarize the outcome, followed by supporting facts and quotes in descending order of importance, and ending with the least important details. It originated in the 1840s at the time the telegraph and Morse code were invented to ensure that crucial information was transmitted first in the event there was a technical problem sending the rest of the story. Traditionally, straight news stories and breaking news use the inverted pyramid style. Social media has adapted the inverted pyramid to grab readers' attention and share news stories across social media platforms.

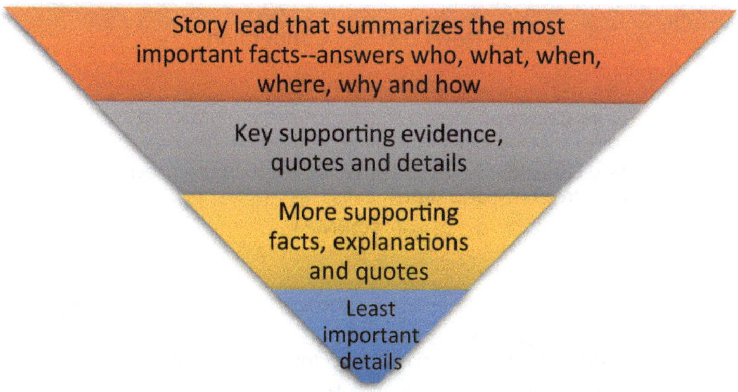

Fig. 5.1: Inverted Pyramid Style of Reporting
Source: Author

Which techniques are best for multimedia storytelling?

Multimedia storytelling offers audiences different ways to engage across multiplatforms. Some formats adapt traditional journalism techniques, while others are native to digital and social media. For example, newsmaker profiles, opinion pieces, personal stories, photo and video galleries might be integrated with animated content, interactive documents, timelines, maps, quizzes and games. Multimedia elements are embedded into the main story text to view graphics and videos while reading the story, or appear to the side at the relevant point in the story, or stacked to the side of the story text to be viewed after reading the main story. Some video-driven stories immerse viewers into a three-dimensional representation of the story in the visual space of the narrative. The goal is to engage news consumers, streamline their experience, especially on mobile devices, and empower them to control how they want to read and navigate the story (Advanced Media Institute, n.d.).

When we are aware of what makes a story newsworthy, how a news story is constructed, and the techniques used to tell the story, it helps us understand the best way to "read" the story.

Ask the Right Questions: Format

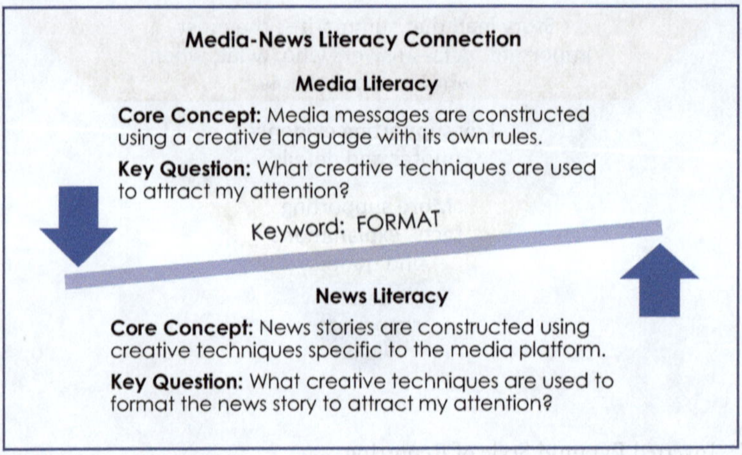

Fig. 5.2: Keyword — Format
Source: Author

Key Takeaways

1. News stories are constructed using creative techniques that have distinct characteristics specific to the technology — whether the story format utilizes text, graphics, photography, audio, video, animation, or multimedia depends on the print, electronic, digital or streaming platform.
2. Certain creative techniques are used to attract audience attention to more newsworthy stories such as large, bold or catchy headlines, prominent

story placement, compelling graphics, live coverage, audio or video, multimedia, hashtags, tweets and retweets.

3. The most common storytelling technique for straight news is the inverted pyramid style that begins with the most important facts and ends with the least important. Opinion, investigative, and feature stories use techniques to best tell those stories. Stories written for digital media use innovative multimedia formats to attract audience attention and make it easier to read on mobile devices.
4. As the news media ecosystem transforms the way we get news, what makes a story newsworthy is not changing — newsworthiness depends on news values, editorial judgment, and audience interest.
5. Universal news values drive the newsworthiness of a story — the more news values driving a story, the more prominent the coverage, and the more attention it potentially receives from the audience.
6. News stories are constructed using common style guidelines for grammar and language, and story elements that include a beginning, middle and end, lead, headline, dateline, byline, photo caption, nut graf, and source attribution.
7. Journalists strive to identify their sources but in certain circumstances use anonymous sources who are known to them but not disclosed to the public.

Guiding Questions

- Why is this story newsworthy? Why might the audience be interested in the story? Consider the prominence of who is involved, timeliness, importance, and magnitude of the event, its relevance and proximity to people, focus on conflict or change, something of human interest or an unusual or odd happening.
- Which media technology and format are used to tell the news story? How are traditional formats like print, TV, radio, and photography similar or different from digital formats like a podcast, meme, GIF, tweet or other social media post in telling the story?
- What creative choices were made to construct the news story? Which storytelling technique and text, visual or audio cues are used? How does the story construction and newsworthiness affect the story placement, amount of news space, and choice of media platform?

- Do the headline and graphics match the story or are they used to attract interest, get "likes" or serve as clickbait to evoke strong emotion? Is the story the original content or has it been digitally altered or previously published elsewhere and made to appear current?
- How is the source attributed? Is the source on the record, off the record, on background or not for attribution? Does the source attribution make the story more or less credible? Why?

Reflect: How do the limitations or advantages of the media technology, story format, and storytelling technique affect the newsworthiness and credibility of the story?

References

Advanced Media Institute. (n.d.). Taxonomy of digital story packages. University of California, Berkeley Graduate School of Journalism. https://multimedia.journalism.berkeley.edu/tutorials/taxonomy-digital-story-packages/

Clark, R. (2019, August 13). "Lead" vs. "lede": Roy Peter Clark has the definitive answer, at last. Poynter. https://www.poynter.org/reporting-editing/2019/lead-vs-lede-roy-peter-clark-has-the-definitive-answer-at-last/

Clark, M. (2016, June 27). It's time for a new set of news values. Here's where we should start. Poynter. https://www.poynter.org/newsletters/2016/its-time-for-a-new-set-of-news-values-heres-where-we-should-start/

Digital Resource Center. (n.d.). The universal news drivers. Center for News Literacy, Stony Brook University. https://digitalresource.center/content/universal-news-drivers

Mast, J., & Temmerman, M. (2021). What's (the) news? Reassessing "news values" as a concept and methodology in the digital age. *Journalism Studies, 22*(6), 689–701. https://doi.org/10.1080/1461670X.2021.1917445

6 Do News Media Take Sides?

Do news media take sides? It seems like a simple question, but the answer is not that straightforward. It is about the nature of objectivity and truth in journalism, the transparency of the news-gathering process, the evidence that demonstrates the story is fair and balanced and not biased, and the bias news consumers bring to reading, watching or listening to news.

Is News Objective?

The nature of objectivity is a thorny issue. When it comes to objectivity, can anyone truly be objective? Probably not. Just as we all carry our biases with us, so do journalists. But there is one big difference. Objectivity in journalism is not entirely about journalists being free of bias; rather, it is that journalistic practices are objective and unbiased. Objectivity is about the method of reporting the truth based on the facts, not the objectivity of the journalist. Journalists are expected to approach their work without personal or cultural bias and acknowledge it when there is, and apply a consistent method that is transparent, free from personal and financial conflicts of interest, and tests the veracity and accuracy of the information before publishing the story.

To ensure that journalism practices are as objective as possible, media outlets and professional news associations around the world have developed codes of conduct for ethical journalism practices that share five core principles: *truth and accuracy, independence, fairness and impartiality, humanity, and accountability* (Ethical Journalism Network, n.d.). Journalists are obligated to tell the truth and strive for accuracy in getting the facts right. To act independently and not beholden to special interests except the public's right to know. To provide balance, add context and report the story fairly without prejudicial images or loaded language. To balance the public's need for information against potential harm to sources, the issue in question, colleagues and the public. To be accountable and transparent and publicly correct errors and take responsibility for them.

Ten core principles of journalism

Over the years, journalists in the United States have developed a common understanding of good journalism practices based on 10 essential principles. These principles originated in 1997 as the Statement of Shared Purpose, drafted by the Project for Excellence in Journalism's Committee of Concerned Journalists, and became the basis for the seminal book by Bill Kovach and Tom Rosenstiel, *The Elements of Journalism*. These essential principles of journalism practices and responsibilities have endured and are more important than ever in the Digital Age of Disinformation when many Americans distrust the news, demonize journalists, and lack the skills to distinguish facts from falsehood. These are the 10 core principles (American Press Institute, n.d.):

1. *Journalism's first obligation is to the truth.*
   Journalists are obligated to pursue the truth in their reporting to ensure that citizens have reliable and accurate information to make informed decisions in a democracy.
2. *Its first loyalty is to citizens.*
   Journalists' loyalty is to all citizens, not just those who have privilege of wealth or education.
3. *Its essence is a discipline of verification.*
   Journalists must use methods to gather and verify facts that are objective and transparent.
4. *Its practitioners must maintain an independence from those they cover.*
   Journalists must be independent of overt partisanship, religious affiliations, and opposition to any groups.

5. *It must serve as an independent monitor of power.*
Journalists must serve as a watchdog to monitor those whose power and position most affect citizens.
6. *It must provide a forum for public criticism and compromise.*
Journalists have a responsibility to provide a forum that fairly represents the diversity of views and improves the quality of debate in society.
7. *It must strive to make the significant interesting and relevant.*
Journalists must report significant stories in interesting and relevant ways to balance what the audience wants with what they need.
8. *It must keep the news comprehensive and proportional.*
Journalists must be inclusive and respect diversity of backgrounds and perspectives in their reporting.
9. *Its practitioners must be allowed to exercise their personal conscience.*
Journalists must be allowed to act on their personal sense of ethics and encouraged to speak their minds.
10. *Citizens have rights and responsibilities.*
Social media has empowered citizens with the ability to share information widely when they comment on social media, blog, tweet or retweet, and "like" an image or a post. Unlike journalists, citizens do not have to be concerned with objectivity or truth or fairness or balance. Yet journalists have to be concerned with the veracity of the information that citizens share and help them prioritize and differentiate reliable from fraudulent information that daily flood their digital devices. Always at the core of journalism practices is the pursuit of truth.

What is journalistic "truth"?

"Is it true?" That is one of the most critical questions news consumers should ask about a news story. How does a news consumer know if the story is true? The answer to this question begins with an understanding of what journalistic truth is.

When the Project for Excellence in Journalism's Committee of Concerned Journalists developed the core principles essential to the practice of journalism, the very first principle is about truth: "Journalism's first obligation is to the truth." Journalism is a truth-gathering process. Journalists seek to report the truth by gathering and verifying facts and putting them into a meaningful context for readers to make their own judgment about the information. If new information surfaces that is verified and changes an earlier version of the story, journalists revise the story and explain why. Journalists are transparent about what they know, what they don't know, and what more they need to know. This applies to any story, especially breaking news. When a story is fast developing, the news report will indicate that it is a developing story to let news consumers know that they should follow the story to get the latest facts. Truth in journalism is said to be provisional because the facts may change as new information becomes known.

What exactly is provisional truth?

At its core, journalistic truth is provisional truth subject to change as new evidence emerges. It is the "best obtainable version of the truth" at that time based on the evidence (Mullin, 2017).

Journalists are very much like scientists in pursuit of truth. Both journalists and scientists are expected to approach their work without preexisting beliefs and biases, apply objective methods to gather evidence, and draw conclusions based on observable facts they verify and determine are reliable. Like scientists, journalists start by observing what is happening and ask the same questions: who, what, when, where, why and how? They provide a context to describe and explain what has happened and are transparent about their sources, the method for gathering the information, and any new evidence they find. Just as scientific truth changes as the evidence changes, journalistic truth changes as more evidence becomes available and the story is revised to report what is known to be true at the time.

To ensure that the evidence is objective and reliable, both the scientific and journalistic methods have self-correcting mechanisms built into the research and publication process to control and verify the findings. In the same way that scientific studies are peer reviewed before publication, news stories are reviewed by other journalists for accuracy before and after publication. If a story is not verifiable by several sources, journalists are obliged to gather more information to ensure it is accurate. If an article is published and found not to be accurate after publication, then the journalist and the news organization will correct it and publicly take responsibility. In journalism, while truth may be provisional, it is evidence-based provisional truth.

How Is the Story Framed?

A news story is an account of an event that presents a view of reality. It reconstructs the event from a particular perspective. The same news story can be told from different angles. The angle or perspective is called a story frame. The way the story is framed affects how it is researched and reported, who is interviewed and the questions that are asked, which quotes and photographs are used, and how the information is interpreted by the reporter. Even the headline frames the story from a certain angle. Essentially, the story frame is the way the information is presented by journalists and understood by news consumers.

Think of a frame in terms of a photograph. When we take a photograph, we choose a subject in our field of vision and frame the image in the viewfinder. We make choices about the focal point, lighting, filters, distance and depth. If we change the photographic composition, it changes the viewpoint. The visual components capture a particular perspective of the image in the same way the narrative elements present a particular angle of the story. Just as the outcome of a photograph is a result of certain choices made by the photographer, a news story is a product of the storytelling choices made by the journalist.

How journalists choose to frame a story defines the context and guides the way news consumers interpret the story and understand the event or issue. When we read a news story, we tend to assign more importance to the more salient aspects of the story. If we only look at the headline, how it frames the story is how we understand that issue or event. What is included or omitted and what is emphasized or deemphasized in the story or headline influences our interpretation of the event, shapes our attitudes and opinions, and can reinforce and perpetuate stereotypes. Ultimately, how the story is framed affects the way we think, act and feel about people, issues and events reported in the story.

What are the different story frames?

Journalists use a variety of storytelling frames. The choice of frame depends on the type of story and the best way to tell it. The most common frame is the *straight news account* that does not have a dominant narrative frame and instead presents the facts: who, what, when, where, why and how something happened. Other frames focus on conflict or consensus, track winners and losers, expose wrongdoings or injustice, provide a reality check, explore a policy, focus on a person's reaction to what occurred, explain how something works or relates to a larger trend or historical perspective, conjecture about the future, or profile a personality. These frames were originally identified by the Project for Excellence in Journalism (Pew Research Center, 1998) in a study to explain why a news organization covers a story and the narrative approach journalists use to compose the story.

News Story Frames
Straight news account: Answers the basic 5Ws and H — who, what, when, where, why and how?
Conflict: Focuses on points of contention, a power clash, a political battle, a sports rivalry
Consensus: Emphasizes points of agreement about an issue among persons, groups or organizations with a vested interest
Conjecture: Speculates about what might happen in a situation or process taking place now
Story: Explains a process or how something works and provides historical context if needed
Outlook: Compares a current event to what happened before
Horse race: Explains who or what is perceived as winning or losing in a political campaign, policy debate, athletic event or other situation
Trend: Spotlights what is trending in the news
Policy explored: Examines the impact of a policy
Reaction: Spotlights a major player's response to events
Reality check: Examines the veracity of a situation or what a reporter accepts as truth or falsity of a particular statement
Wrongdoing exposed: Reveals an injustice, misconduct, illegal or criminal activity
Personality profile: In-depth look at a newsmaker

Is the Story Fair, Balanced or Biased?

How do we know if a news report is fair and balanced? Or if a news outlet is biased? Look for the evidence. The evidence tells us if the reporting is fair, if the story is balanced, and if the coverage is biased. But what does it mean to be fair, balanced or biased? Let's start with some definitions.

What is fairness?

Fairness is about being truthful and honest about the evidence. Fairness is not taking sides or making judgments. Fair reporting is impartial and independent, without prejudice, bias, favoritism or self-interest, and does not omit anything important that would affect how the public makes sense of the story. Three key factors contribute to determining the extent to which a news story is fair or unfair: *fair language, fair presentation, and fair play.*

Is the language fair? Fair language means being fair to the coverage in the choice of words used to report about the issue, people or institutions. Fairness is using neutral verbs such as "said" or "told" instead of "admitted" or "disclosed" and words that are not loaded with politically partisan language. For example, "undocumented immigrant" instead of "illegal alien" or "marriage equality" instead of "gay marriage" or "unhoused" instead of "homeless."

Is the presentation fair? Fair presentation is about the choice of visuals to tell the story — photographs, videos, illustrations, charts and graphs. If a story is fair, then there are no prejudicial photos or videos, misleading charts or graphs, deceptive illustrations, and all visuals are relevant to the story.

Is there fair play? Fair play is an obvious effort in the news reporting to include all relevant perspectives and allow an opportunity for newsmakers, organizations and institutions to respond to any criticism or negative coverage in the story.

Is the story balanced?

Fairness can require balance. *Balance* is a matter of mathematics. It is a quantitative measure of news coverage. If a story is balanced, then all sides of the issue are covered equally. Equal amount of space in the newspaper or equal length of time in the newscast. Presenting a balanced perspective is particularly important for a developing story or when something is unknown, unclear, undetermined or undecided.

Are there always two sides to a story?

There are not always two sides to a story. Then how is the story reported? When the facts are clearly one-sided, balance is not fair. In these instances, if journalists try to create balance, then what they really are doing is creating a false equivalency. A *false equivalency* is news coverage that is not fair to the evidence. It is when the reporting presents an issue as more balanced than the evidence supports.

A good example of false equivalency is climate crisis (Grimes, 2019). Scientific evidence leaves no doubt about the catastrophic effects of global warming and has discredited so-called "experts" who deny the science of climate change. If a news report presents the opposing views of climate deniers as equally credible as climate scientists, then the coverage is not accurate or truthful and is a false equivalency. While this example is false balance, is it biased?

How do we know if there is bias?

Bias is not based on one news story. *Bias* is based on many news stories that consistently demonstrate a pattern of unfairness over time. If a news outlet's coverage of a prominent person or hot-button issue is predominantly negative, inaccurate or one-sided, then that news outlet is biased against that person or issue. Bias might be headlines, story angles or photos that consistently skew coverage of a politician and what that person represents in unfavorable ways.

What bias is not is important to recognize. Bias is *not* news that does not agree with our point of view. Just because news coverage does not support our viewpoint does not mean it is biased. Bias is *not* opinion journalism. Opinion journalism, by definition, is subjective because it expresses the writer's viewpoint based on verifiable facts, transparency about conflicts of interest, and accountability for any errors. Bias is *not* advertising. Advertising is paid placement of a message in order to increase brand recognition and sell a product or service.

The Missing White Woman Syndrome

Have you noticed that pretty, young, white women go missing? Don't Black, Brown and Indigenous women disappear? Why don't we hear more about these cases? Is the coverage biased?

Missing white woman syndrome — a term coined by Gwen Ifill, an award-winning journalist who broke barriers as a Black female reporter and news anchor — refers to the media frenzy surrounding cases involving attractive and youthful white women who have disappeared, been kidnapped or murdered compared to the relative lack of media attention to non-white women.

The missing white woman represents the damsel in distress who captivates the nation with front-page headlines, prime-time news segments, news alerts and press conferences, and social media photos, videos, and postings speculating about the circumstances. The repeated lack of coverage of missing non-white women signals that they are not valued as much as white women. Media bias is a pattern of unfairness. This disparity clearly is biased coverage.

Where's the Evidence?

Evidence provides proof that the facts in a story are accurate and true. The nature of the evidence indicates the extent to which the reporting is fair, balanced or biased. Not all evidence is equal. Evidence differs in its strength and reliability.

What are the different types of evidence?

Accuracy and verification are based on a *hierarchy of evidence.* The strongest and most reliable is *first-hand direct evidence* that can establish a fact: a source related to the story, photographs, audio and video recordings, documents and records, eyewitness testimony, DNA, fingerprints or other physical evidence. Next is *second-hand indirect evidence* such as an account from a person who is knowledgeable about the situation but not directly involved or computer models and other types of expert reconstruction. Journalists always look for direct evidence, especially when second-hand evidence is an off-the-record account or from a spokesperson such as a lawyer, press agent or press release, hearsay testimony or inferences drawn from the evidence.

Journalists need evidence to get the story right. Sometimes the verification process fails even with the evidence. There are several reasons why. One reason is that journalists want to scoop other journalists and be the first to report the story. In the rush to get the story, they may get something wrong. Another reason is that journalists might be up against a deadline to finish the story and not have all the details before the newspaper edition is published or the newscast airs. Yet another reason is a journalist's source might not have been correct or truthful about information they provided for the story. Lastly, if the journalist does not speak the language and needs a translator, something might literally get lost in translation.

"If your mother says she loves you, check it out."
This is an old newspaper adage that means journalists should be skeptical but not cynical and question everything. Never assume anything — even if the source is a trusted one like your mother (Scanlan, 2003).

The news-gathering process begins with the facts. Journalists need to attribute and corroborate every fact so they do not get a story wrong and have to correct it later. But the facts alone are not enough. Facts need to be put into context to provide perspective. Facts should describe and explain the circumstances so that news consumers can fully understand and assess what is happening. To protect the integrity of the news-gathering process, journalists are transparent about how they gather the facts, what questions could not be answered and why, what information might be questionable or contradictory. Transparency is especially important when there is a breaking story about a developing crisis and there is a sense of urgency to get accurate information quickly to the public. In these circumstances, it becomes more difficult to verify each piece of information as it dribbles in and more critical to explain what is verified and why certain information cannot be verified in order to provide a context for the public. So, if your mother says she loves you, she probably does, but where's the evidence?

Whose "Fault" Is It?

Everyone has their "faults." That is, fault lines or blind spots when it comes to race, class, gender, generation, geography, education, religion, politics, disabilities and other differences. When we meet a person for the first time, we tend to make assumptions about that person based on how they fit preconceived categories of difference we construct in our minds. And people make assumptions about us based on how we align with the social categories they construct in their minds. These are fault lines that limit our perception and can lead us to misperceive who a person really is. Fault lines can also spark microaggressions toward people who are perceived as members of culturally marginalized groups that are frequently stereotyped, discriminated against, and victims of prejudice. These prejudicial insults and affronts happen in casual and business situations, often without any harm intended, and creep into online communities in comments, posts, tweets, memes and GIFs on social media.

The concept of fault lines originated from Robert Maynard, the first African American editor of the *Oakland Tribune* and founder of the Maynard Institute for Journalism Education. He used the metaphor of geological fault lines that cause the earth to rupture to describe social fault lines that can fracture societal structures and relationships. The original Fault Line Framework focused on race, class, gender, generation and geography because Maynard believed these five underlie the most prevalent social tensions since our nation was founded. The framework has become a tool for journalists to be aware of their own fault lines and more deeply examine the issues, images and sources in their reporting. The goal is to attempt to relieve stress points between groups and more accurately report stories by recognizing bias and accepting natural differences rather than ignoring them (Lehrman, n.d.; Maynard Institute, n.d.).

How do fault lines affect our news perception?

As news consumers, we want news content to mirror the makeup of our community, whether it is based on race, ethnicity, gender, sexual orientation, social class, religion or politics. We want to see ourselves and hear our voices on the pages of newspapers and websites, in newscasts and podcasts, and on social media where we get news. Like journalists, we have our own fault lines that kick in when we read, watch or listen to news. We first need to acknowledge and confront our own fault lines to recognize the fault lines reflected in a journalist's choice of news angle, sourcing, language and images to report the story. When we accept that we have these biases, we can begin to "correct" our vision and understand how others might perceive, misperceive or misinterpret people, issues and events. Start by asking some questions: How are fault lines represented in news? Are journalists transparent about their fault lines? How do those fault lines affect ours? Do media reinforce or disrupt them? The answers to these questions can help us understand why we choose certain news outlets over others or follow certain journalists for their reporting or commentators for their opinions.

Whose fault line is it?

Social media enables us to connect and interact in ways never before possible and, at the same time, emboldens the spread of discrimination and social injustice beyond the five original fault line social tensions — race, class, gender, generation, and geography. As social tensions gradually emerge in society, they become more complex. Consider how social tensions happening in the world and reported in the news extend the fault line framework.

Social tensions caused by racial prejudice often trigger prejudices related to ethnicity and nationality as well. High, middle and low income do not fully capture class status. While not technically a social class rather a social class phenomenon are unhoused individuals. Gender includes gender identity and sexual orientation. Common generational categories of 0-18, 19-34, 35-64, and 65+ may be too limiting to define seniors who are working and living longer. Geography is no longer confined to urban, suburban, rural or neighborhood type and encompasses red states and blue states and regions of the world.

Other social tensions have become salient fault lines: religious differences and opposing political ideologies have polarized the nation. Education has become more divisive. Ableism and disability discrimination is widespread yet often overlooked. Acknowledging fault lines gives voice to differences and deepens our understanding of one another.

Do News Media Take Sides or Not?

Journalism strives for the free exchange of information that is truthful, accurate, impartial, fair and balanced, and provides context based on evidence grounded in facts and attributed to sources. Journalistic objectivity requires that:

- ✓ journalists do not take sides on an issue
- ✓ journalists do not create a false balance when the issue is clearly not two-sided
- ✓ journalists check their personal and cultural biases and political and religious affiliations at the gate and not allow them to influence their journalistic objectivity
- ✓ journalists report only the facts, unless it is an opinion column, and then it is their opinion based on the facts
- ✓ journalists are transparent about their conflicts of interest, accountable for their reporting, and publicly correct reporting errors when they occur

Journalists have the responsibility to use their forum to encourage public discussion that fairly represents the diversity of views in order to inform and empower citizens to responsibly participate in democracy. If journalists practice these ethical principles, then news media do not take sides. However, in today's climate of hyper-partisan politics, if it appears to news consumers that there is a bias in the way the news is framed, then the journalist or news outlet might very well be driven by ideology and partial to one side of an issue over another. Or news consumers may bring their own bias to interpreting the news. Then the question for news consumers becomes, who is your gatekeeper?

Ask the Right Questions: Content

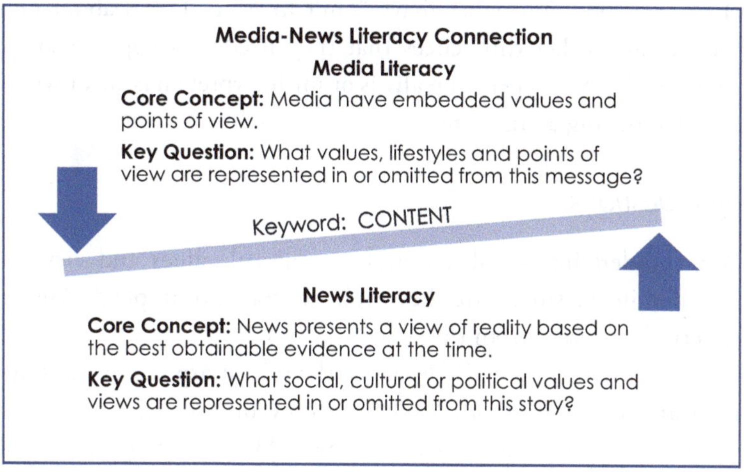

Fig. 6.1: Keyword — Content
Source: Author

Key Takeaways

1. News is an account of an event that presents a view of reality and provides a meaningful context to understand what is happening in the world.
2. Journalism is a truth-gathering process based on the best obtainable evidence at the time. It is called provisional truth — as new evidence emerges, the story will be revised to reflect the facts.
3. Journalists first obligation is to report the truth using a consistent method that is transparent about how they gathered and verified the facts, interviewed their sources, and discovered any new evidence.
4. Journalism practices around the world are guided by professional codes of ethics that share core principles — truth and accuracy, independence, fairness and impartiality, humanity, and accountability.
5. Journalists use different story frames that depend on the type of story and the best way to tell it. How a story is framed can affect the point of view and social, cultural, and political values represented in the story.
6. Journalists and news organizations strive to be fair in their reporting and balanced and unbiased in their coverage, unless balance would present a false equivalency.

7. The accuracy and verification of a story is based on a hierarchy of evidence. The strongest and most reliable is first-hand direct evidence such as an eyewitness account, audio or video recordings or physical evidence.
8. Like everyone, journalists have "fault lines" or biases about race, class, gender and other differences that they need to recognize so as not to misperceive who a person really is or misinterpret an issue or what is actually happening at an event.

Guiding Questions

- What underlying social, cultural or political values and viewpoints are included in the story? Are they explicitly stated or implied? Are any views selectively omitted from the story?
- How is the story framed? What are the salient aspects of the story? Does the frame fit the story or mispresent the event or issue?
- What is the evidence? Is it clearly shown? How accurate and reliable is the evidence? Is it first-hand or second-hand evidence?
- Are the choice of words used to characterize the event, issue or newsmaker neutral and free of loaded language? Is the overall presentation fair? Are selected images appropriate and not prejudicial?
- Is the coverage fair, balanced and unbiased? Are all relevant perspectives represented? Or is the reporting one-sided or hyper-partisan? Does the coverage present a false balance because the opposing side is not equally valid? Are facts put into context? Are conclusions reasonable or based on flawed logic?

Reflect: What is your responsibility to check the quality of the information you share on social media? How do you know if a news story is fair, balanced and unbiased? How do you know if the evidence is accurate and credible? Do you check multiple, trustworthy sources?

References

American Press Institute. (n.d.). *Journalism essentials.* https://www.americanpressinstitute.org/journalism-essentials/what-is-journalism/elements-journalism

Ethical Journalism Network. (n.d.). *Our five core principles of ethical journalism.* https://ethicaljournalismnetwork.org/who-we-are

Grimes, D. (2019). A dangerous balancing act: On matters of science, a well-meaning desire to present all views equally can be a Trojan horse for damaging falsehoods. *EMBO Reports, 20*(8), e48706. https://doi.org/10.15252/embr.201948706

Kovach, B., & Rosenstiel, T. (2021). *The elements of journalism* (4th ed.). Crown.

Lehrman, S. (n.d.). Diversity toolbox: How to cross your 'faultlines.' Society of Professional Journalists. https://www.spj.org/dtb2.asp

Maynard Institute. (n.d.). Fault Lines. https://mije.org/diversity-training/fault-lines/

Mullin, B. (2017, April 30). Read Carl Bernstein and Bob Woodward's remarks to the White House Correspondents' Association. Poynter Institute. https://www.poynter.org/reporting-editing/2017/read-carl-bernstein-and-bob-woodwards-remarks-to-the-white-house-correspondents-association/

Pew Research Center. (1998). *Framing the news: The triggers, frames and messages in newspaper coverage.* Project for Excellence in Journalism. https://www.pewresearch.org/journalism/1998/07/13/frame/

Scanlan, C. (2003, April 17). If your mother says she loves you: A reporter's cautionary tale. Poynter Institute. https://www.poynter.org/reporting-editing/2003/if-your-mother-says-she-loves-you-a-reporters-cautionary-tale/

7 Who Is Your Gatekeeper?

Who determines the news you get? Do you, or a news outlet, or a social media site, or someone else? What news we get depends on the "news gates" we choose. News gates are different points of entry where we can access news and information in the media environment.

Traditionally, the major news gatekeepers who decide which stories are important have been mainstream newspapers, news magazines, television and radio news. That is no longer the case. The digital media landscape has multiplied the number of news gates and at the same time empowered news consumers to become their own gatekeepers. Instead of solely depending on news media gatekeepers, news consumers are increasingly becoming part of the gatekeeping process by filtering stories from the stream of information they encounter and sharing them online.

No matter where we get our news, we will come across many of the same stories but with different messaging. The difference might be the headline, lead, news angle, storytelling technique, photograph, source attribution, word choice, or the context and evidence used to support the facts. These differences, even subtle ones, can change the meaning of the message. Which news gatekeepers we choose really matters because of two important reasons. First, the stories gatekeepers select to report prioritize our personal agenda of issues we think are important. Second, the way gatekeepers frame a story can shape our worldview, affect our understanding of issues, and influence our opinions, attitudes and behaviors.

When the news agenda becomes our agenda, it affects people differently. Think about it this way: no two people interpret the same message in the same way. How we understand news messaging depends on our individual experiences, our prior knowledge about the topic, our preexisting opinions, attitudes, values, beliefs, and biases — both conscious and unconscious biases, especially confirmation bias that drives us to depend on news outlets and online communities that reinforce our views. And, of course, our critical thinking and news media literacy skills affect our understanding as well.

The best way to explain how different people might interpret and respond to the same news messaging is through relevant research and theories. Four media-related theories provide a context to understand how news influences the public agenda and our personal news agenda, cultivates our social reality, triggers a willingness to express our opinion or remain silent about an issue, and affects our perception that others are more susceptible to believing "fake news" than us.

Who Sets the News Agenda?

Agenda setting is about power — the power to shape our perceptions of the world. This is the power to influence which issues we should think about and, in some circumstances, how we should think about them. The mainstream news media have long controlled this power until social media networks fundamentally changed the way the public keeps informed.

The widespread use of social media networks for news has fragmented the power and shifted it away from the established news outlets toward news consumers who no longer rely solely on traditional media for their news. Instead, news audiences choose news from various media and other sources, including mainstream news outlets. They may turn to news aggregators, alternative news sites, talk shows, podcasts, community forums and social media, along with friends and family. They decide for themselves what is "news" and blend the various agendas based on their individual needs, interests, and personal values. This is called agenda melding. Whether the news agenda is set by mainstream news media or a process of agenda melding, the agenda setting effect is a powerful effect that can determine which issues should concern us and what we know about them.

What is the agenda-setting effect?

News outlets cannot possibly cover everything that is happening in the world and instead prioritize the importance of the events for their audiences. News editors and reporters choose which issues and events to emphasize, deemphasize others, or omit them altogether from their news coverage. The issues given more news coverage will be the ones we think are important, and the way the news story is told will determine what we know about the issue and influence how we think about it. News media's ability to select and emphasize certain issues influences our perception of the importance or salience of these issues and affects our attitudes and opinions about them. Essentially, the *agenda setting effect* is the transfer of salience from the news media's agenda to the public's agenda on issues that resonate with them. How does the process of agenda setting apply in the digital media environment? The answer is best understood by explaining the evolution of agenda setting theory.

Agenda setting theory has a long history of scholarship starting with the landmark study by Maxwell McCombs and Donald Shaw (1972) about the powerful role media play in shaping public opinion. In this study, they analyzed how news coverage affected voters' perceptions of the salient issues in the 1968 U.S. presidential election. They found that the issues news media emphasized in its coverage matched the issues the public perceived to be important. The more attention given to an issue, the more the public perceived the issue to be important and influenced what they should think about. What drives agenda setting is people's *need for orientation* to their environment, especially if they have an interest in the issue or some uncertainty about it. Since the initial study, there have been hundreds of agenda setting studies conducted in the United States and internationally. This growing body of research shows how agenda setting theory has evolved with the changes digital technology has brought to the media landscape and the ways people access news. The evidence is clear: the new digital media forms play just as important a role as traditional print and broadcast in setting the public and policy agendas (McCombs & Valenzuela, 2021).

The notion of agenda-setting was first articulated by the renowned American journalist Walter Lippmann. Often called "The Father of Modern Journalism," Lippman drew the connection between news coverage of events and the images people have in their minds of those events. While Lippmann did not use the term agenda setting, McCombs credits him with being the forefather of the concept. In his book entitled *On Public Opinion,* published in 1922, Lippmann essentially described how the agenda-setting function of the press affects people's perception of the world and its impact on public attitudes. Lippmann explained that through the news media we come to know a world that we do not directly experience, yet we accept it as a true picture of reality and it shapes our worldview. He called the world constructed by news media the *"pseudo-environment"* and contended that this pseudo-reality, which tends to stereotype specific groups, influences the *"pictures in our heads"* of our perception of the world. The "pictures in our heads" are a reflection of media's edited version of reality and not necessarily what is actually happening in the world. Nevertheless, these pictures affect what we think we should be concerned about and, in turn, influence public opinion.

McCombs conceptualization of agenda-setting theory was further advanced by political scientist Bernard Cohen in his book *The Press and Foreign Policy.* In the early 1960s, Cohen observed (1963, p. 13):

> The press is more than a purveyor of information and opinion. It may not be successful much of the time in telling people what to think, but it is stunningly successful in telling its readers what to think *about*… the world looks different to different people depending not only on their personal interests, but also on the map that is drawn for them by the writers, editors, and publishers of the paper they read.

Initially, agenda-setting theory posited that media tell us what to think about rather than influence how we should think about it. Later research reconceptualized this statement because studies found that the news not only *tells us what to think about* by focusing our attention on the issue, but *how to think about it* by constructing the story in a certain way — deciding what facts and opinion to include and emphasize, who to quote, which photo and camera angle to use.

When the concept of the "pictures in our heads" originated at the beginning of the 20th century, newspapers were the main news source that shaped people's perception of the world. In the 21st century, there are many more media that contribute to our picture of reality besides newspapers — magazines, TV, radio, documentaries, movies, video games, podcasts, websites, apps, social media networks, and emerging media forms yet to be named. In the media ecosystem, we tend to meld together a variety of news agendas, some are from standards-based news organizations while others are from sources that may not apply journalism standards and practices. Some of these sources might be imposter sites or promote conspiracy theories, hoaxes or pseudoscience, or contain deepfakes or other types of disinformation. This is very worrisome because if the "pseudo-environment" is based on disinformation, then the "pictures in our heads" may very well reflect a false narrative. Nevertheless, our subsequent actions have real consequences that may be harmful to others or to the democratic process when they play out in the real world.

What is the difference between agenda setting and agenda melding?

While *agenda setting* is about media's ability to choose which issues are important to the public, *agenda melding* is about news consumers' ability to select which media and stories are important to their individual needs and interests and blend the various agendas for themselves (McCombs et al., 2014). Agenda setting is an inadvertent byproduct of the news process. News editors and reporters decide which stories to focus on and how to tell the story. They apply editorial judgment and journalistic practices to gather, prioritize and report the news and, in the process, focus audience attention on issues they determine are newsworthy for the public's understanding of the world. News gatekeepers' ability to emphasize certain issues can influence which issues the audience thinks about. Large, bold headlines, a photo or graphic accompanying the story, an editorial endorsement, prominent story placement — especially the front page above the fold or top of the scroll, or the lead story on the newscast, or the stories highlighted on a newsfeed — are cues that signal to the audience the salience of the story.

Agenda melding is a more active process that empowers the audience as news consumers, extends their community of friends and experts, and provides a context to make sense of the news. News consumers actively control their news consumption and pick and choose from among multiple agendas to build their news agenda that can change with each social interaction. Their picture of the world is a mix of the various media they use, groups they join, and people with whom they interact, melding news agendas from mainstream news organizations with websites, blogs, podcasts and social media that fit their needs and interests to create meaning for themselves.

When we combine agendas, where we get news may or may not apply standards-based journalism practices and instead may be purveyors of false and misleading information. Tweets, retweets, posts, tags, and likes can make an issue appear to be salient and focus attention on it, but the quality, reliability and relative importance of the information may not be apparent. Then how do we know if the news story is evidence-based, independent and transparent in its reporting, or disinformation that needs to be debunked? We need to be our own fact-checkers or rely on group discussions to verify the information. There is some evidence that blending and building an agenda by discussing news in groups may be a viable strategy for increasing news media literacy among young adults (McWhorter, 2020). This is important especially in instances in which news consumers rely less on traditional gatekeepers and more on "gatewatchers" whose group agenda has the power to influence the public agenda.

Who are gatewatchers?

Are you a gatewatcher? Do you select news from different gatekeepers and share it with your friends on social media? *Gatewatchers* are news consumers who curate the news for themselves based on their own needs and interests, or those of their community, and share it with family, friends and followers in social media environments (Bruns, 2018). Gatewatchers do not require journalistic skills or subscribe to a code of ethics. Instead they need basic Internet search skills to gather news and information and use their own judgment to decide what is credible and newsworthy. To some extent, this undermines traditional gatekeeping control by news outlets that use journalistic criteria to assess the facts and determine the newsworthiness of a story. Some have asked, does gatewatching mean the end of gatekeeping? The answer is yes and no. While the shift from gatekeeping to gatewatching has weakened the gatekeeping function, news organizations have also benefitted from gatewatching. When gatewatchers repackage and share news stories, news outlets get their stories more widely disseminated.

What is the difference between news gatekeepers and gatewatchers?

It is the difference between the *Fourth Estate* and the *Fifth Estate* and who *publishes verses publicizes* the news. *Gatekeepers* are professional journalists who work for conventional news organizations that gather and publish the news. *Gatewatchers* are online users who curate, share and publicize the news on networked social media platforms. Gatekeepers are part of the Fourth Estate and serve as democracy's watchdog uncovering truths and falsehoods and holding the government accountable to the public. Gatewatchers are networked individuals and self-organizing communities enabled by the Internet that are part of the Fifth Estate and serve as an alternative to mainstream media. Some are motivated to newsshare for self-serving reasons such as a sense of self-worth or the status it brings them, while others share because they genuinely think the information is important for their family, friends and followers to know (Bruns, 2018).

Any news consumer who habitually compiles and shares news stories on a social media platform is a gatewatcher. Citizen journalists are a type of gatewatcher who post online and bypass traditional outlets to report or comment on a news story. Some gatewatchers are part of online communities where users collaboratively gatewatch, filter and publicize news relevant to their interests that was originally published elsewhere by professional journalists or publicized by citizen journalists or other social media users. They take on the role of editor selecting content and deciding whether an article, opinion piece, video, photograph, meme or other material is important or interesting enough to recommend. They may participate in discussions about the news and add commentary or analysis on their social network as a way to contribute to public discourse outside of the Fourth Estate. The agenda that gatewatchers create can shape their followers understanding and view of the world as much as the agenda prioritized by media gatekeepers can influence the attitudes and opinions of their readers, viewers and listeners.

How Might Different People Understand the Same News Story?

Just as different news media report the same story with different messaging, different news consumers understand the same story in different ways. Why? The simple answer is there is no one way to interpret anything. Two people can read the same news article or social media comment, watch the same news broadcast, TV show, movie or video, listen to the same song, podcast or talk show, or observe the same advertisement and understand it very differently. Wherever we get our news, whoever our gatekeeper is, we interpret news stories based on our view of reality. How we view and understand the world depends on our prior knowledge and experiences, personal values, beliefs and biases, as well as how we interpret the multitude of media messages we encounter in our everyday lives.

Think about your view of social reality. What is your conception of the "real" world? When you think about a person or a place or an event, what mental picture do you conjure up based on your personal experiences? We all see the world in our own unique way. The image we construct is from both direct first-hand personal experience and indirect mediated experience based on what we watch, read and listen to in the media.

For most of us, media are a common source about everyday life, culture, politics, and the economy. The more time we spend in the media world, the more media images and messages "cultivate" a real world view that, to a certain extent, aligns with the media reality to which we expose ourselves. We may not even be aware of media's influence on our perception of reality because it happens subtly and slowly over time. This is called the cultivation effect.

What is the cultivation effect?

The *cultivation effect* refers to media's influence on our construction of social reality. Regardless of how different people's backgrounds are from one another, if they are frequently exposed to the same media messages, they will share a common worldview. This common or mainstream view of the world that people cultivate based on their common media experience tends to resonate more with individuals whose real-life experience is congruent with their media exposure. They get a *double dose effect*, media plus their lived experience, which amplifies the cultivation effect. How does the cultivation effect apply to news? A look into cultivation research helps explain how news can shape our social reality about the world and affect different people in different ways.

George Gerbner and his colleagues at the Annenberg School for Communication at University of Pennsylvania (1969) developed the concept of cultivation as the cornerstone of the Cultural Indicators Project in the 1960s to study the social and cultural impact of media representations on society. They wanted to understand how media messages represent the world and affect audiences' conception of social reality. Their focus was television because it was the dominant medium people used for news and entertainment and Gerbner considered it the primary cultural storyteller in our society. At the time there was an increasing level of violence in society after the Civil Rights Movement that was reflected in TV news and entertainment programming. They found that the more a person watched violence on television, the more they perceived the world to be "a mean and scary place" and became fearful of being a victim of violence themselves. Since the initial studies, cultivation analysis has been applied to different forms of media and topic areas, including news, gender identity, minorities, mental health, aging, politics, religion, science and the environment in a range of cross-cultural contexts (Morgan et al., 2015).

In the digital media landscape that has emerged, television is no longer the dominant storyteller that cultivates a mainstream view of the world. Technology has created many more ways to deliver and receive content that has enabled many more storytellers to tell stories and altered the original concept of mainstreaming (Morgan et al., 2015). Instead of one central powerful storyteller that cultivates a mainstream view of the world, there are many sources of storytelling that cultivate many mainstreams with different messaging. The elements of the storytelling may be the same, but the messaging is not.

The cultivation process is more about the content and the meaning audiences make from it than the technology that delivers it (Shanahan & Morgan, 1999). It does not really matter whether the content is delivered via broadcast, cable, satellite, streaming, Internet platform or accessed on a TV set or mobile device. What matters is the underlying content and how audiences interact with it. The intrinsic nature of interactivity in the online environment adds a dimension to the meaning audience's make of a message that is not possible with television. News and personal views can easily be shared with others, many others, accelerating the cultivation effect and creating social media bubbles that enable users to interact with one another about the content. This can have a unifying effect for its members who share common interests and ideological viewpoints or a polarizing effect for those who do not share the same interests and ideologies, especially when it comes to social and political issues.

How does news cultivate our social reality?

News media play a particularly powerful role in shaping our social reality. News helps us simplify the complex world in which we live by constructing a prepackaged narrative that interprets reality for us and, in turn, affects our attitudes, opinions and beliefs, as well as our actions. The digital media ecosystem is potentially an ideal environment for the cultivation effect. From standards-based news outlets, to hyper-partisan news programs, podcasts and radio talk shows, to websites and social media networks, we have many different choices of storytellers. Most of us tend to turn to news storytellers who reinforce our social reality. This can contribute to echo chambers that restrict our worldview, understanding and openness to other viewpoints.

Inside an echo chamber where the same messages repeat and reverberate, confirming people's beliefs and biases, news consumers may share a common view that may be based on facts or on falsehoods and prejudices that can be harmful to others and to society in general. The message will resonate even louder for those whose real-life experiences with friends and family reinforce the same views. For many, a like-minded ideological perspective may also be supported in other online communities and social networks they frequent. When the line between online and offline blends, it strengthens the support for attitudes and opinions expressed in an echo chamber.

Pizzagate: How disinformation can evolve into real-life violence

It is troubling to think that conspiracy theories might cultivate a person's worldview and evolve into real-life violence. That is what happened on December 4, 2016 when 28-year-old Edgar Welch, armed with his assault-style rifle, drove 350 miles from his home in North Carolina to Washington, D.C. During the drive, he recorded a message on his cellphone to his daughters: *"I can't let you grow up in a country that is so corrupt by evil without at least standing up for you and for other children just like you."* What was the evil that Welch felt he had to protect children from and where did he hear about it? He was on a mission to "self-investigate" an alleged child-trafficking ring at a popular pizzeria.

According to Welch's testimony, after binge-watching YouTube videos and listening to Conservative talk show host Alex Jones' radio show about a pedophile and satanic child pornography ring, Welch became extremely upset and set out on a mission to rescue the children. Known as Pizzagate, this baseless conspiracy theory went viral on social media claiming that Hillary Clinton, her campaign chair John Podesto, and other influential Democrats were responsible for a child pornography ring headquartered at Comet Ping Pong in Washington, D.C. When Welch arrived at the restaurant, he parked his car, walked in with a Colt revolver on his hip and a loaded AR-15 in his hand, pointed the weapon at the employees and fired a shot, which luckily did not hurt anyone. After searching the restaurant and finding no evidence of the child abuse, he surrendered to police and was charged with assault with a deadly weapon and sentenced to four years in prison.

This bizarre case demonstrates how disinformation can cultivate a person's social reality. The more Welch watched the videos and read the articles, the more he perceived the country to be, in his own words, "so corrupt by evil." Welch was not the only one who was exposed to this conspiracy theory. Hundreds of thousands of YouTube views and tens of thousands of message board subscribers promoted the false claim that resonated with conspiracy believers. Alex Jones later apologized to the owner of the restaurant for promoting #Pizzagate on his radio show and Infowars website. In court documents, Welch said his intention was to help children who were in danger and realized his action was reckless and apologized to the families and the community for endangering them.

The false online Pizzagate claim lives on in death threats to the restaurant owner and the dangerous conspiracy theories that continue to spread online. Experts who study conspiracy theories call Pizzagate an early warning sign for how disinformation can lead to even greater violence, reach more people, and divide us more as a country, which is exactly what we witnessed four years later with the January 6th insurrection on the U.S. Capitol. [Background about Pizzagate is from *The Washington Post* (Miller, 2021) and *The New York Times* (Aish et al., 2016)].

How media represent the world matters. It matters because media have the power to shape our social reality and influence how we understand our world and act in it. We've seen what happens when fantastical claims dupe us into believing they are true and motivate an individual or a group to take the law into their own hands. What happens if news presents a false balance in reporting critical social issues? What if news covers a complex issue in overly simplistic terms, obscuring what really is important, making us think we understand the issue more than we really do? Might we make judgments or vote on an issue based on incomplete understanding? What happens when we don't see or hear our views? How does this affect our construction of reality, how we feel about ourselves, and the way we experience the world? Might we choose to remain silent and not express our opinions because we fear rejection? That can be explained by the "spiral of silence."

Who's Caught in the "Spiral of Silence"?

How many times might we want to share our opinion, but we don't because we fear rejection? Or we spoke out against a controversial issue and then regretted it because of backlash we received? When this happens, we might be caught in a "spiral of silence."

Whether we realize it or not, we are consciously checking which opinions and behaviors are supported or rejected by the public at large or the group to which we belong. We may remain silent because we perceive our view to be contrary to popular opinion. We tend to be especially unwilling to express our views about politics when the topic is about a polarizing issue or contentious candidate. If we voice a differing opinion, we are afraid of being judged negatively and put down, or laughed at, or ostracized from the group. However, if our views are aligned with the majority, then we are more willing to express our opinion loud and clear. This is called the spiral of silence.

What is the "spiral of silence"?

The *"spiral of silence"* is a term coined by German political scientist Elisabeth Noelle-Neumann (1974) to explain how people's perception of public opinion impacts their personal attitudes and conscious expression of their opinions. She developed the spiral of silence theory to better understand political situations such as the Nazis' rise to power that was made easier by Germans who disagreed with Hitler but remained silent. The theory was initially applied to face-to-face interactions and traditional mainstream media. With widespread use of social media, the digital environment offers new opportunities to express public opinion and expand public discourse. To what extent are people taking advantage of digital interactions to voice their opinions, or are they remaining silent and not contributing to the public conversation on social media platforms? Researchers have begun to re-examine the spiral of silence in the social media world (Hopkins, 2015).

One of the first studies comparing the spiral of silence effect on social media to in-person conversations was conducted by Pew Research Center about a controversial issue that was in the news. The issue was the disclosure of highly classified documents that were leaked by Edward Snowden revealing U.S. government surveillance of American citizens' phone and email records (Hampton et al., 2014). Researchers did not find that social media provided an alternative platform for people who are otherwise reluctant to express their views. What they did find is a similar spiral effect in social media networks as in-person interactions. Facebook and Twitter users were more willing to discuss their opinions on social media and in-person if they thought people agreed with their views. If they thought that social media friends and followers disagreed with their views, they were less willing to express their opinion online as well as offline in conversations with friends, family, and coworkers.

Since the time that study was conducted, more people go online for news and there are more opportunities to engage in public debate and discussion on important political issues. Most of us tend to have go-to news sites, whether it is the digital version of our preferred newspaper, newscast or podcast, or a favorite social media or online community we frequent to stay informed and interact with people who share our views. We can comment on news and interact with journalists at news outlets about their stories. We can be prosumers who not only consume but publicize news by reposting a story or produce messaging by commenting or creating content. Compare that to traditional media where the opportunity for news readers to engage is limited largely to letters-to-the-editor, and even then, not all letters get published. Whether or not we take advantage of the opportunities to speak up publicly depends on the dynamics of the online environment where we get our news.

Do social media silence us or encourage us to speak up?

Social media is a highly interactive environment that empowers anyone with access to the Internet to have a platform to voice an opinion about anything. Why some may choose to be outspoken while others remain silent depends on the circumstances of the interaction.

In the social media world, we can choose to be anonymous or to be known to a network of friends and followers. If we make ourselves known to our list of "friends," presumably they are people who share similar views or interests. Also friend requests are supposedly suggested because of what we have in common. This familiarity may make us more inclined to express our views because we perceive there is support within the community and any opposition to our views is likely to come from outside the group. If we choose to be anonymous, the anonymity may allow us to speak up when otherwise we might keep silent (Meyer & Speakman, 2016).

When we voice our opinion on social media, we can amplify it far more than if we had voiced the same opinion face-to-face. Posting, reposting and retweeting spreads the message quicker, wider and farther to audiences beyond our friends and communities. Because we do not know who will see it and what their reaction will be, we are vulnerable to whatever the consequences are of sharing our viewpoint with unintended audiences. We could be publicly shamed, harassed or bullied by people who disagree with our viewpoint and cause us to retreat into silence or leave the social media network altogether. It is also possible that a minority view with a loud voice may appear to be more widespread and more acceptable on social media than it actually is in mainstream society because it resonates with people who were not the intended audience.

Social media can intensify or weaken the spiral effect in ways that are different than face-to-face interactions. When we interact in-person, we hear tone of voice and observe body language, facial expressions, clothing and hairstyles, and judge whether or not we want to share our opinion. A frown, a smirk, a raised eyebrow, a nod, a smile can signal a reaction and affect our response. In the social media environment, verbal and non-verbal cues are different than in-person exchanges. Instead, digital body language is expressed in videos, photographs, graphics, memes, GIFs, emojis, sound effects, filters, along with text devices that we intentionally choose for emphasis when we want to draw attention to what we have to say. There are also calculated emotional appeals of propaganda and conspiracy theories targeted to audiences who will spread them online. And there are personal attacks, which social media emboldens, directed at news organizations, journalists, politicians, government officials, and thought leaders in an effort to silence them or damage their reputations. These tactics can increase or decrease our willingness to express our views online. Elected and appointed officials who receive threats to harm them and their families may decide to resign or not run for office, and journalists, who are supposed to report the news unemotionally and not become the subject of the story, may be provoked when personally attacked and express their emotions.

The nature of social media is community. We join different communities based on our interests and ideologies. These are smaller self-contained communities — *information silos* — that have their own spirals and can insulate us from other viewpoints. While we tend to think of the Internet as a public space where a diversity of expression exists that can foster healthy debate necessary to advance democracy, these smaller communities can cultivate a single point of view and prevent that debate from happening.

Think echo chambers. Echo chambers reinforce strong opinions on one side and silence unfavorable opinions on the other side. If we stay within our echo chamber where our views are supported, the spiral is exaggerated. We think everyone has the same views and opinions, which further reinforces the views we share with them. Staying within this community, we may miss important information that might change our minds about an issue, or we may be unwittingly exposed to false and misleading information, including conspiracy theories, rumors and hoaxes. If we do change our view, we may opt to keep it to ourselves for fear of retribution from the group or we may leave the group entirely. Because if we express a view that is not widely shared, then we could suffer the consequences. We might be overwhelmed by negative comments or publicly shamed in tweets and retweets, comments and posts that may go viral and carry over into real world situations.

How does news coverage affect the spiral effect?

How journalists cover a news story can influence our perception of public opinion on the issue, person or event that the story is about and, subsequently, impact the spiral effect. If the media favors one side over another of a highly debated issue, then the favored side may be perceived as the prevailing public opinion.

If our viewpoint is the one that is favored, then we may think that a majority of people share our view and we are more likely to speak out and take action to support it. But if we do not share the predominant view, we might believe that people do not agree with our viewpoint and we are less likely to voice our opinion or engage in discussion about the issue.

This is logical thinking but may be a misjudgment of the news coverage. It is possible that the lack of coverage is more about newsworthiness than about not supporting our viewpoint. The editors at the news organization may simply not consider the story to be interesting enough or relevant to its audience. Or there may not be a valid opposing viewpoint that warrants coverage and providing one would be promoting a false equivalency. The alternative view may not be supported by a legitimate expert or grounded in empirical evidence and may be based on fraudulent information. It is also possible that we might perceive a minority view as the majority view because its supporters are outspoken in defending their viewpoint and determined to share their message widely.

Cancel culture and the spiral effect: The case of Justine Sacco

In the Digital Age, anyone who has access to a platform can be a publisher whether it is a blog post, Instagram story, TikTok video or a Twitter thread. Social media has a way of emboldening people to express an opinion that they might not say in person. What happens when we voice our opinion but are publicly shamed by people who are offended by our views? We may be silenced or "canceled" by our own doing. When we share a comment on a public platform, we don't know who is watching or what their reactions will be and how it will ultimately affect us. The Internet is a public space with invisible audiences that potentially have the collective power to ostracize individuals and even ruin someone's life. While the term cancel culture applies more to celebrities and public figures, it aptly describes what happened in the well-publicized public shaming case on social media that became the subject of an international news story and a book entitled *So You've Been Publicly Shamed* (Ronson, 2015).

Justine Sacco was on her way from New York to South Africa via London to visit family for the Christmas holiday. She was 30 years old and a senior executive at a major corporate communications company. When she boarded a plane in New York, she started tweeting sarcastic comments about the trip to her 170 Twitter followers: *"'Weird German Dude: You're in First Class. It's 2014. Get some deodorant.' —Inner monologue as I inhale BO. Thank God for pharmaceuticals."* Then on her layover at Heathrow she posted: *"Chilly — cucumber sandwiches*

— bad teeth. Back in London!" And before she left on her 11-hour flight from London to Cape Town, she tweeted: *"Going to Africa. Hope I don't get AIDS. Just kidding. I'm white!"*

When she arrived at her destination, she turned on her cell phone while taxiing to the terminal and checked her messages. First she saw a text from someone she had not spoken to since high school that read: *"I'm so sorry to see what's happening."* Then another text from her best friend: *"You need to call me immediately."* Her Twitter feed exploded with tens of thousands of angry tweets and the hashtag #HasJustineLandedYet was trending on social media.

She was publicly shamed about her perceived bigotry and racist ignorance and fired from her job. Her words did not support values shared by her community and had dire consequences. She became a victim of online vitriol and threats, a cautionary tale of controversial unchecked remarks on a public platform. She says that her tweet was taken literally and out of context. What happened to Justine? After being publicly fired from her job, she volunteered in Ethiopia, returned home to a position in corporate communications, and is staying out of the Twitter spotlight (Blanchfield, 2015). We tend to think that something like this can happen to other people but not to us — that media affects others more than it affects us. Or does it? That can be explained by the "third-person effect."

Who Is the "Third Person"?

Could the "third person" be you? Most of us believe that media messages influence other people more than ourselves. That is to say, media do not impact "me" or "you," but it does affect "them." Them, or other people, are the third person. The truth is we may be more influenced by media messages than we think we are.

Many of us tend not to think that ads influence our buying preferences for brand name products. Or models and celebrities with perfect body shapes make us want to look like them. Or playing violent video games affects our aggressive tendencies. Or that we might unwittingly spread a rumor, hoax or conspiracy theory. But we perceive that other people are influenced by advertising, ideal body shapes, violent video games or "fake news." Unlike "me" and "you," we think that others are more susceptible to media's influence because they lack the knowledge and skills to resist these messages. This is called the third-person effect.

What is the "third-person effect"?

The *third-person effect* predicts that people tend to underestimate media's influence on themselves and overestimate its influence on others (Davison, 1983). Our perception that media has a greater influence on others than on ourselves is affected by certain factors. One is perceived similarity — that is, the social distance that we perceive exists between us and them. If we perceive ourselves to be similar to other people, then we do not think they will be influenced that much by media. But people we perceive as being not like us will be affected by media. That means our closest group of friends and family or people in our social network who are like us will not really be affected, while people who are not in our social network, or the general public who are not like us, will be influenced a lot.

Another factor is our self-perceived knowledge about the media message. Often the more we think we know about something, the more we think persuasive media messages do not affect us while the same messages can affect others. Yet another consideration is the media message itself. If we perceive a media message to be socially undesirable, even harmful, or that it might reflect negatively on us if we admit to believing it, then we are likely to think that other people are more susceptible to the message's influence than we are or people we know. Our perception of media's influence on others might motivate us to respond or take action to protect others from harmful messages. On the other hand, if we perceive a media message is socially desirable, then there might be a *first-person effect*. That means that we are likely to think that the positive message will affect us more than others, especially if it is consistent with our views and the views of our friends and social groups (Perloff, 2009).

Who Believes "Fake News" — Me, You or Them?

When it comes to news, we tend to perceive people who pay attention to news as being well-informed and educated. That includes ourselves. What about "fake news"? Do we perceive that we are not influenced by false stories that pose as legitimate journalism, or conspiracy theories, or pseudoscience, or real news that politicians call "fake news" because it is not favorable to them? While a majority of people are concerned that "fake news" is causing confusion about the facts and could undercut an informed citizenry, they do not think that everyone is susceptible to "fake news." They generally feel confident in their ability to identify "fake news," despite that some admit to spreading "fake news" (Pew Research Center, 2016).

The third-person effect plays a role in how people respond to "fake news" and perceive its impact on themselves and other people. Here are a few things we know. People who underestimate the influence of "fake news" on themselves and overestimate its influence on others tend to be confident in their own ability to detect false news reports and feel strongly that others fall for "fake news" but they do not (Cheng & Chen, 2020). Social media users in particular overestimate their competency in spotting "fake news," despite that people who use social media have not been found to be more skilled than others in detecting fraudulent information. They perceive "fake news" on social media as socially undesirable and are concerned about its harmful effect on others (Yang & Horning, 2020).

What do social media users think we should do to protect people they perceive as vulnerable to the effects of "fake news"? A priority is media literacy education. Social media users advocate for teaching digital media literacy skills to learn to critically evaluate media in order to identify and combat "fake news." They also think that corporations should take responsibility to correct falsehoods, even if the corporation is a victim of the false news story (Cheng & Chen, 2020). Instead of government action to curb "fake news" in the media ecosystem, social media users support self-censorship of their own newssharing to protect others on social media they perceive to be susceptible to "fake news." They are willing to self-censor by decreasing their newssharing and not sharing either "fake news" or "real news" online or talking about it offline. Researchers warn that this could have an unintended consequence on lessening the flow of accurate and inaccurate information and, in turn, political debate and discussion (Yang & Horning, 2020).

"Fake news" often is politically charged and has a polarizing effect. It is not surprising that political party affiliation plays a role in the third-person effect. People perceive that "fake news" especially impacts voters who are affiliated with a political party other than their own. A study (Jang & Kim, 2018) that analyzed Republican versus Democratic voters found that Republicans believed that "fake news" influences Democratic voters more than themselves or other Republican voters. Democratic voters perceived that Republican voters are more vulnerable to "fake news" than themselves or other Democratic voters. This partisan third-person effect was even greater among voters who more strongly identified with their party. Researchers caution that this could lead to a false impression that information shared by members of our own political party is accurate and true when it may not be.

Might a third-person effect inhibit the spread of "fake news" on social media? That is yet to be determined. Since most people get their news from social media and social media is where "fake news" is most widespread, the best defense is digital media literacy education. We need to get into the habit of applying news media literacy skills to access, analyze, and evaluate news and information, create content using all forms of communication, and take action to disrupt disinformation and promote quality journalism.

Ask the Right Questions: Audience

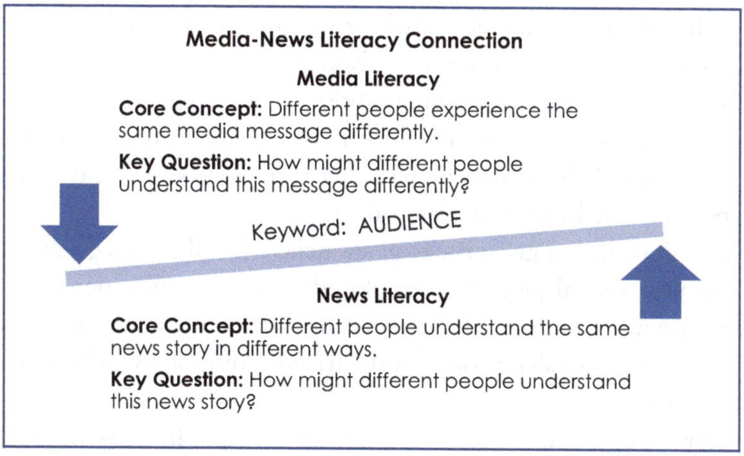

Fig. 7.1: Keyword — Audience
Source: Author

Key Takeaways

1. There is no one way to interpret a news story — different people understand the same news story in different ways. We interpret news based on our prior knowledge and experiences, personal beliefs and biases, and preexisting attitudes and opinions.
2. Unconscious bias can reinforce stereotypes, limit our worldview, and affect how we interpret and react to a news story — especially confirmation bias that reinforces our existing beliefs and can trap us in a filter

bubble or confine us to an echo chamber that we trust and depend on for news and information.

3. Where we choose to get our news matters because news gatekeepers play a powerful role in shaping our social reality by telling us what is happening in the world. As part of the news-gathering process, gatekeepers select and prioritize issues and events they decide are important for the public to know creating an agenda setting effect.
4. The agenda-setting effect refers to news media's ability to choose and emphasize certain issues and events and, in turn, the public perceives them to be the ones that are important to think about, and can also influence how the public thinks about them. When different news outlets report the same news story with different messaging, particularly with a political slant, it can have a polarizing effect on the public agenda.
5. As more people get their news from social media, the power of agenda setting has shifted away from traditional gatekeepers at news outlets to an agenda melding process in which news consumers decide for themselves what news is important by blending various news agendas that fit their personal needs, interests, and values.
6. Social media has given rise to gatewatchers. Unlike news gatekeepers who are professional journalists employed at news organizations, gatewatchers are news consumers who constantly watch the news gates and curate news stories to share with family, friends, and followers in social media communities.
7. News media can influence our agendas about which issues should concern us, cultivate our social reality, and affect our response to what is happening in the world — we may take action or be less willing to speak out on an issue, or perceive that other people are more influenced by a news story than ourselves, even if it is "fake news."

Guiding Questions

- How might different people understand the same news story? How does a person's knowledge, attitudes and opinions affect their understanding of a news topic? How might they interpret the story based on their age, race, ethnicity, gender identity, education, social class, political ideology or where they live? How many interpretations could there be?

- How might people's confirmation bias affect their news choices and understanding of a news event? What actions might someone take based on conclusions they draw from a story that supports their bias or challenges it?
- How do you know who the target audience is for a news story? Check where the story appears, who wrote or posted or commented on it. In what ways might news consumers "read" a story shared on social media differently from one they get directly on a mainstream news outlet?
- What is the difference between a gatekeeper and a gatewatcher? How do gatewatchers impact gatekeepers? Are people more likely to encounter disinformation if they get their news from gatekeepers or gatewatchers?
- What is the agenda setting effect? How does agenda setting influence people's view of the world? In what way does agenda melding limit or expand news consumers' worldview?
- What circumstances might affect someone's willingness to express their opinion or remain silent on an issue presented on social media or discussed in person? How does news coverage affect the spiral of silence effect?
- Who do people perceive to be most susceptible to "fake news" — themselves, family and friends, or people they don't know? What do social media users think we should do to protect people who are susceptible to believing "fake news"?

Reflect: Who's your gatekeeper? Is your gatekeeper an echo chamber? How do your biases affect why you choose certain news gatekeepers over others, how you interpret a story, and the information you share? Have you or someone you know ever shared "fake news" and what happened? What circumstances might encourage you to express your opinion or keep silent about your views?

References

Aish, G., Huang, J., & Kang, C. (2016, December 10). Dissecting the Pizzagate conspiracy theories. *The New York Times*. https://www.nytimes.com/interactive/2016/12/10/business/media/pizzagate.html

Blanchfield, P. (2015, February 24). Twitter's outrage machine should be stopped. But Justine Sacco is the wrong poster child. *The Washington Post*. https://www.washingtonpost.com/posteverything/wp/2015/02/24/twitters-rage-mob-should-be-stopped-but-justine-sacco-is-the-wrong-poster-child/

Bruns, A. (2018). *Gatewatching and news curation* (Digital Formations, vol. 113). Peter Lang Publishing. https://eprints.qut.edu.au/215471/

Cheng, Y., & Chen, Z. (2020). The influence of presumed fake news influence: Examining public support for corporate corrective response, media literacy interventions, and governmental regulation. *Mass Communication and Society, 5,* 705–729. https://doi.org/10.1080/15205436.2020.1750656

Cohen, B. (1963). The press and foreign policy. Princeton University Press.

Davison, W. (1983). The third-person effect in communication. *Public Opinion Quarterly, 47*(1), 1–15. https://doi.org/10.1086/268763

Gerbner, G. (1969). Toward "cultural indicators": The analysis of mass mediated public message system. *AV Communication Review, 17,* 137–148. https://www.jstor.org/stable/30217499

Hampton, K., Rainie, L., Lu, W., Dwyer, M., Shin, I., & Purcell, K. (2014, August 16). *Social media and the 'spiral of silence.'* Pew Research Center. https://www.pewresearch.org/internet/2014/08/26/social-media-and-the-spiral-of-silence/

Hopkins, A. (2015). Effects of the 'spiral of silence' in digital media. *Inquiries, 7*(9), 1–2. http://www.inquiriesjournal.com/articles/1104/effects-of-the-spiral-of-silence-in-digital-media

Jang, S., & Kim, J. (2018). Third person effects of fake news: Fake news regulation and media literacy interventions. *Computers and Human Behavior, 80,* 295–302. https://doi.org/10.1016/j.chb.2017.11.034

Lippmann, W. (1922). *On public opinion.* Harcourt, Brace & Co.

McCombs, M., & Shaw, D. (1972). The agenda-setting function of mass media. *Public Opinion Quarterly, 36*(2), 176–187.

McCombs, M., Shaw, D., & Weaver, D. (2014). New directions in agenda-setting theory. *Mass Communication and Society, 17*(6), 781–802. https://doi.org/10.1080/15205436.2014.964871

McCombs, M., & Valenzuela, S. (2021). *Setting the agenda: Mass media and public opinion* (3rd ed.). Polity.

McWhorter, C. (2020). The role of agenda melding in measuring news media literacy. *Journal of Media Literacy Education, 12*(1), 145–158. https://digitalcommons.uri.edu/jmle/vol12/iss1/11/

Meyer, H., & Speakman, B. (2016, April 14). Quieting the commenters: The spiral of silence's persistent effect on online news forums. *International Symposium on Online Journalism, 6*(1). https://isoj.org/research/quieting-the-commenters-the-spiral-of-silences-persistent-effect-on-online-news-forums/

Miller, M. (2021, February 16). Pizzagate's violent legacy. *The Washington Post.* https://www.washingtonpost.com/dc-md-va/2021/02/16/pizzagate-qanon-capitol-attack/

Morgan, M., Shanahan, J., & Signorielli, N. (2015). Yesterday's new cultivation, tomorrow. *Mass Communication and Society, 18,* 674–699. https://doi.org/10.1080/15205436.2015.1072725

Noelle-Neumann, E. (1974). The spiral of silence: A theory of public opinion. *Journal of Communication, 24,* 45-31. https://doi.org/10.1111/j.1460-2466.1974.tb00367.x

Perloff, R. (2009). Mass media, social perception and the third-person effect. In J. Bryant & M. Oliver (Eds.), *Media effects: Advances in theory and research* (3rd ed., pp. 252–268). Routledge.

Pew Research Center. (2016). *Many Americans believe fake news is sowing confusion.* https://www.pewresearch.org/journalism/2016/12/15/many-americans-believe-fake-news-is-sowing-confusion/

Ronson, J. (2015). *So you've been publicly shamed.* Riverhead Books.

Shanahan, J., & Morgan, M. (1999). *Television and its viewers: Cultivation theory and research.* Cambridge University Press.

Yang, F., & Horning. M. (2020). Reluctant to share: How third person perceptions of fake news discourage news readers from sharing "real news" on social media. *Social Media + Society*, 1–11. https://doi.org/10.1177/2056305120955173

8 Digging Deeper

Fact-based journalism. Opinion. Satire. Sponsored content. Clickbait. Conspiracy theories. Deepfakes and cheapfakes. All types of news and information indiscriminately follow us wherever we go in the media ecosystem blurring the line between real news, opinion, advertising, entertainment, made-up and manipulated content. This has fueled an information crisis that has created confusion and controversy further polarizing the country. One person's facts are another person's conspiracy theory. Americans' inability to agree on what is true and what is false poses a real threat to democracy.

Of course, there have always been and always will be differences of opinion, but there are not "alternative facts." Truth matters. The First Amendment guarantees freedom of the press because it is critical to democracy that news organizations function as watchdogs to ensure that the government is accountable to its citizens. Journalists investigate the evidence and report the facts to inform citizens about current events so that they can actively and responsibly participate in democracy based on a shared understanding of reality. To quote Daniel Patrick Moynihan, former ambassador, senator, and adviser to four American presidents: "Everyone is entitled to his opinion, but not his own facts" (Weisman, 2010, p. 2).

We may want to place blame for the maelstrom of disinformation on algorithms, bots and chatbots, or foreign bad actors, but the truth is that we humans are superspreaders (Gersema, 2020). Some spread it unknowingly, and others intentionally. Confirmation bias, filter bubbles and echo chambers have a lot to do with unwittingly spreading disinformation, while an agenda of deception deliberately disseminates fraudulent information for personal, economic, and political gain. Undeniably, there are many factors that contribute to the erosion of truth in the public sphere. The question is, *what are we willing to do about it?*

Solutions range from controlling news and social media content by clearly labeling the content for what it is and flagging disinformation to alert the reader or viewer — identify it as opinion, satire, conspiracy theory or other disinformation type — to educating students and the public about news literacy. We can label and flag content, which will certainly help, but if we wish to stop feeling the effects of disinformation being weaponized against democracy in our public spaces, we need news media literacy education to empower ourselves as lifelong learners who can differentiate truth from lies. It starts with knowing how to ask the right questions to critically evaluate the evidence, fact-check the facts, compare multiple news sources from varying perspectives, read beyond the headlines, and be aware of the different types of mis/dis/malinformation. How do we dig deeper to find the facts, identify false and inaccurate news and information, and disrupt disinformation?

No More CRAAP!

Navigating around the different types of mis/dis/malinformation can be challenging and even a bit risky. It takes critical thinking skills to be mindful and wary of *all* information we come across. We need to be ever-watchful of inaccurate or false and misleading information that has crept into every corner of the Internet. This fact-checking process can be exhausting, but well worth the effort to ensure that what we read, hear and see is reliable and credible and that we do not contribute to the spread of disinformation.

There are a variety of strategies to assess the trustworthiness and value of information, and some are better than others to disrupt the complex nature of the disinformation disorder. One of the methods that is widely used to teach students to evaluate the reliability and credibility of information is called the CRAAP Test. This test was developed by a librarian at California State University, Chico (Blakeslee, 2004) prior to social media's dominance as a source for news and information and is limited in its application to the interconnected network of information that has evolved since that time.

What is the CRAAP Test?

CRAAP is an acronym for Currency, Relevance, Authority, Accuracy, and Purpose. Currency is the timeliness of the information. Relevance is the importance of the information depending on its purpose. Authority is the source of the information. Accuracy is the correctness, reliability and truthfulness of the information. Purpose is the reason why the information was created.

CRAAP is essentially a checklist of questions to evaluate the website where the information originates. The basic questions ask: How timely is the information? How relevant is the information for its purpose? Who created the information? How factual is the information? Why was the information created? These questions are valuable for a close reading of a source but can lead to trusting information that is unreliable or biased or dismissing information that is credible. What's missing is context. In the dynamic network of information that is continuously evolving on the web, context is essential for evaluating nuanced information to determine its authenticity, credibility and motive, especially user-generated content and digitally manipulated text, images, audio and video that flood our social media feeds.

Beyond CRAAP

Some educators are adapting the CRAAP method to fit a more immersive fact-checking experience, while others advocate retiring this method altogether in favor of strategies that dig below the surface for a deeper critical contextual evaluation (Wineburg et al., 2020). Still others propose more proactive evaluation strategies that reframe the focus on our experience navigating the increasingly networked information environment that is driven by algorithms programmed to find its users across multiple platforms. According to this approach, to proactively navigate the digital infrastructure, we need to understand how information finds us wherever we go online, where it comes from, the impact of algorithms and strategies to circumvent them, and ways to build our own networks of trusted sources to search and verify information (Bull et al., 2021).

In the networked online world where we are left on our own to filter fact from opinion and fiction, we need innovative skills to be our own gatekeepers to find quality, reliable and trustworthy information and strategies to help disempower and mitigate the influence of mis/dis/malinformation. That means ditch the checklist, get off the website, and search like a fact-checker.

How to Search Like a Fact-Checker

Educators are turning to professional fact-checkers to help students become critical consumers of news and information in an increasingly complex digital media ecosystem. How do fact-checkers research and verify claims? They start by asking three essential questions: *Who is behind the information? What is the evidence? What do other sources say?* To answer these questions, fact-checkers use the techniques of lateral reading, click restraint, and reverse image search, along with other digital tools to verify text, images and videos. This strategy is outlined in the Civic Online Reasoning curriculum developed by the Stanford History Education Group (n.d.) and summarized in a shorthand method based on this approach called SIFT (Caulfield, 2019). *So how do you read laterally, practice click restraint, and SIFT information*?

What is lateral reading?

Lateral reading is a fact-checking process that involves verifying the information as we are reading it by getting off the website to check what other sites and resources state about the same information. It entails opening multiple tabs in the browser to search for information about the nature of a website, why and when content was created, the author's credibility, intent and bias, and the trustworthiness of the information.

The key difference between lateral and vertical reading is the technique used to evaluate the trustworthiness of the information online. Lateral reading is a much deeper reading experience than reading vertically. When we read vertically, we stay on the website and move up and down to assess the source, its authenticity and credentials, the accuracy and purpose of the content, and the design and functionality of the site. For example, if we want to find out who the source is, we click the "About" page on the website and do not leave the website to further check the source for potential affiliations and sponsors that might bias the perspective and question the reliability of the content.

When we read laterally, we evaluate information by getting off the website to search for background and context about the source and check the reliability, credibility, and value of its content. We leave the site and move from tab to tab, opening a new tab to read what other trustworthy sources say about the website owners, creators and authors, and to check the content for accuracy, dates for currency, and hyperlinks to and from the site for the quality of its connections and any affiliations or sponsorships. By the time we are through, we have opened multiple tabs in our browser and read multiple sources to evaluate the original source and the evidence.

Fact-checkers use a variety of lateral reading tools including keyword searches, fact-checking websites, and Wikipedia. Yes, Wikipedia. Although not considered a quality source to cite for research because it is user-generated — not all entries meet editorial standards of accuracy and transparency or policies for posting neutral points of view and substantiating claims — fact-checkers turn to Wikipedia to jump-start the lateral reading process. It is one of the most trafficked websites with billions of unique topics in hundreds of languages that include in-text citations to verify its claims. It is a good place to check out basic information, an unfamiliar website, the credentials of an expert, organization, journalistic source or publication, and find references to further fact-check.

What is click restraint?

When we search online about a topic, page after page of search results appear on our screen. Which one do we choose first? Most of us choose the first or second or third entry at the top of the list on the first page. These choices are not always the most trustworthy and, in fact, they might be sponsored content. Sources are not ranked by trustworthiness but rather by algorithms that analyze the pages based on hundreds of criteria developed by people who work for search engine companies. The quality of the source in the search result is only as good as the quality of the search engine's criteria. It may not be completely objective because it is subject to human error and bias of the people who create the ranking system. So how do we find a reliable source? One way is to practice click restraint.

Click restraint is a strategy to resist the urge to click the first search result and instead pause and take a step back to scan the results and make an informed decision about where to start. Before clicking on a link to a site, make sure to select keywords carefully and check the titles and content snippets to find out who is behind the information. Then click on a few links to compare the results using lateral reading to check their trustworthiness.

What is SIFT?

A simple way to help quickly judge the quality of a digital source is the SIFT method (Caulfield, 2019). SIFT is an acronym for Stop, Investigate the source, Find trusted coverage, Trace claims, quotes, and media back to the original source. It involves four moves that use web tools to guide the process. First, determine your purpose and make a plan for investigating the source. Second, investigate the source by reading laterally to check what others say about the source, the author's expertise, and the accuracy of the content. Third, conduct a more in-depth investigation to find trusted reporting or analysis of different viewpoints on the topic to determine the extent to which the claims are supported. Fourth, trace back to the original source to determine whether the information is accurately reported and used in its original context or in a way that changes the intended meaning. If the SIFT method determines the quality of the information is not acceptable, move on and find a better source.

How to Disrupt Disinformation

There is so much misinformation and disinformation in the digital world that it is not surprising that we might be taken in by some and even "like" or forward it to our family, friends, and followers. Or that someone in our life is a disinformation superspreader and their beliefs result in a rift in our relationship with them. Disinformation has created a divisive news credibility crisis that demands action by all of us. We have a responsibility to not spread false and misleading news and information.

What can we do? Get into the habit of fact-checking what you read, hear and see online. But don't stop there. There is more we can do to disrupt disinformation. It may be time to have a conversation with a family member, friend, co-worker or online acquaintance about "alternative facts." Start with these basic tips.

Find the facts

Dig deep for the answers to the three questions that fact-checkers ask: *Who is behind the information? What is the evidence for their claims? What do other sources say about the person, group or organization and its claims?*

Read laterally and check multiple sources.

As you read, fact-check what you're reading with multiple sources. Open a new tab in the browser. Then another one. And another. Read what other trusted sources say about the source, author expertise, and accuracy of the information. Separate facts from opinion, evaluate the trustworthiness of the data or documents, corroborate conflicting information, and check the links to see where they lead. Ask yourself if the evidence is supported, the context is appropriate, and the facts add up. If you get stuck or hit a dead end, start over again.

Practice click restraint.

Before you click, examine the search results with a critical eye. Don't open the first result. Or the second one. Or even the third. These just might be clickbait or sponsored content. Check the URL, read the snippet of information about the site, and select carefully to find the facts that will increase your understanding of the topic and verify the information.

Search Wikipedia.

Use Wikipedia as a start point and not an end point, primarily for citations. Determine the quality of the information by navigating around the page — check for warnings about the content and "view source" for its protected status. For editable pages, "view history" shows the edits in chronological order and has an option to compare any two revisions. "Talk" in the navigation bar takes you to an administrator page where editors discuss improvements to articles.

Search keywords.

Don't spend too much time on a site. Navigate around the site to confirm its legitimacy and use Ctrl-F to quickly find keywords to guide your fact-checking. If it is not the original source, conduct a keyword search to find it and continue with lateral reading.

Conduct a reverse image search.

To check the authenticity of an image or video, use a reverse image search such as Google Images, TinEye or WeVerify. Dig a little deeper to investigate whether something actually occurred at the location, date and time with the people said to be involved using a *geolocation search* such as Google Earth or other mapping software.

Look for the blue checkmark.

To verify that a social media account of a public figure or global brand is the official one, look for the blue checkmark next to the name. The intention is to prevent impersonation of an elected representative, celebrity or well-known brand or influencer. Be aware that the checkmark can be misused by imposters to create a fraudulent account and spread false and misleading information for devious reasons. Scrutinize accounts with checkmarks before you trust them.

Check with the fact-checkers.

Check fact-checking websites for previous fact-checking about the information. Professional fact-checkers may have already done the work for you. Duke University Reporters' Lab maintains a database of current fact-checking sites.

Read beyond the headlines.

If you want the facts, read the article. Headlines highlight a certain point of the story and do not provide context or evidence needed to make informed decisions. They are written to capture our attention and don't always match the story — even legitimate news outlets can have a misleading headline. If a headline makes you upset or angry, check the source before you react. Be suspicious of sensational headlines — chances are they're clickbait or other type of disinformation. Clues to false or fabricated stories are in the article and not the headline. Before you decide to "like" or share an article, read it!

Find out who owns a website.

Knowing who owns a website can help identify the person or group that created a bogus website or spread a conspiracy theory. There are several free online databases — such as WHOIS and ICANN — where you can search for the domain owner's name and email, registration date and registry expiration. If the domain owner added a privacy option to their registration, then you will not be able to find the information. Question why a website is listed as private or anonymous or is created for a short period of time to spread a specific message, especially around political campaigns and elections.

Report disinformation.

When you encounter any type of false or misleading information, report it to the social media platform after you verify it is untrue. The reporting feature is usually in the Help Center on the site.

Choose trustworthy gatekeepers.

Take a close look at the gatekeepers that influence your ideas. Ask yourself why you chose them and if they are an echo chamber that confirms your biases and beliefs. Make sure to follow gatekeepers committed to ethical standards and practices of quality journalism, read multiple sources that you trust to get different viewpoints, and check your confirmation bias at the gate.

Start a conversation

Fact-checking alone may not be enough to disrupt disinformation. Use your news literacy skills to talk to someone you know who may not have all the facts, believes false or misleading information, or relies on untrustworthy news sources. This may be an uncomfortable conversation, so before you start, fact-check the information, assess the story elements, and plan your approach.

Choose the right time and tone for the conversation.

Create a space to have a meaningful conversation. Try to talk in person or video chat so that you can respond to facial and body language as well as tone of voice. Use supportive language and a positive tone.

Be patient and listen with respect.

Listen to what is important to them and don't be dismissive of their beliefs. Don't put them down or shame them by saying "You're wrong" or "I told you so." To make sure you heard them correctly, paraphrase what they said and ask them if you got it right.

Ask questions that encourage critical thinking.

Do your research but don't attack with facts. Ask questions that prompt them to reflect on what they know, how they know it, and what they don't know. When they bring up untruths, introduce doubt and encourage them to question their beliefs and be open to other views: *Where did you get this information? Why do you believe it is true? What's the evidence? Could there be another explanation? Have you read or heard other points of view or checked what different experts say about it?*

Create a teachable moment to unravel the falsehood.

Be transparent about what you know and how you know it. If you've shared false information, tell them your personal story. Explain how you check sources for accuracy. Show them your newsfeed and compare it to theirs. Help them understand the information environment and how algorithms track and shape what we see on our screens and create filter bubbles that generate revenue for social media. Make them aware of chatbots and other new technology that can auto-generate news but do not always get it right — the information may be biased, inaccurate, plagiarized or entirely false, possibly with the intent to spread disinformation.

Keep your emotions in check.

Avoid confrontation — the intention is not to win an argument. If the conversation escalates, stop and take a break. This can be a difficult dialogue and you may not change someone's mind but you can try to understand their motivation for believing the information and help them see different points of view. Don't give up — keep listening and talking because every little bit helps to move the conversation forward.

Now What?

You assessed your news habits. You checked your filter bubble. You determined if you're in an echo chamber. You examined your confirmation bias.

You know what news is and why news literacy matters. You know how vital the Fourth Estate and the First Amendment are to a democracy. You understand that you need to keep informed to participate responsibly in democracy and that where you get your news matters.

You know how to find news that is reliable and credible. You recognize that news published by gatekeepers at quality news organizations generally is more trustworthy than news curated and publicized online by gatewatchers.

You know who is a journalist and who is not. You understand that journalists are trained in the craft of journalism, grounded in professional codes of ethics, and obligated to tell the truth, verify the facts, disclose any personal or financial conflicts of interest, and if they make a mistake, take responsibility to publicly correct any errors in their reporting.

You realize that journalistic truth is provisional truth based on the best obtainable evidence at the time. You understand that as new information becomes available, journalists will update the story and provide context to understand it.

You understand that whether something happening in the world becomes a news story depends on its newsworthiness, the news judgment of the editor or producer, and audience interest. You know that there are different ways to tell a story and that the storytelling technique depends on the type of news story and media platform where the story appears.

You know how to discern the difference between news and opinion and between journalism and other types of information — propaganda, publicity, advertising, entertainment, and user-generated content on social media. You also can recognize the various types of mis/dis/malinformation and understand that the difference between them is the intent to deceive or harm.

You know how to read laterally, practice click restraint, search keywords and conduct a reverse image search to find the facts and disrupt disinformation. You even know how to start a conversation with someone who has fallen into the disinformation rabbit hole.

When you "read" the news, you know the right questions to ask: What's the purpose of the news item? Who constructed or shared it? Why is the story newsworthy? What storytelling techniques are used? Is the story fair, balanced and not biased? Where's the evidence? Which values and viewpoints are represented or omitted and why? How might different people understand the same story? What does the story mean to me?

You are ready to start using your news literacy skills to burst your filter bubble, escape your echo chamber, and keep your confirmation bias in check whenever and wherever you get your news.

Now that you have the tools to think like a journalist and search like a fact-checker, please pass them along.

References

Bull, A., MacMillan, M., & Head, A. (2021, July 21). Dismantling the evaluation framework. *In the Library with the Lead Pipe.* https://www.inthelibrarywiththeleadpipe.org/2021/dismantling-evaluation/

Blakeslee, S. (2004). The CRAAP test. *LOEX Quarterly, 31*(3), article 4. https://commons.emich.edu/loexquarterly/vol31/iss3/4

Caulfield, M. (2019). Sift (The four moves). https://hapgood.us/2019/06/19/sift-the-four-moves/

Gersema, E. (2020, December 1). How Americans can help stop fake news. *USC News.* https://news.usc.edu/179176/how-to-help-stop-fake-news-misinformation-usc-experts/

Stanford History Education Group. (n.d.). Civic online reasoning curriculum. https://cor.stanford.edu/

Weisman, S. (Ed.). (2012). *Daniel Patrick Moynihan: A portrait in letters of an American visionary.* Public Affairs.

Wineburg, S., Breakstone, J., Ziv, N., & Smith, M. (2020). *Educating for misunderstanding: How approaches to teaching digital literacy make students susceptible to scammers, rogues, bad actors, and hate mongers.* Working Paper A-21322, Stanford History Education Group, Stanford University. https://purl.stanford.edu/mf412bt5333

A Final Word

This book was written during a particularly tumultuous period in our history. I started it at a time of uncertainty and fear during a global public health crisis that changed our way of life — the way we work, learn, play, communicate and interact with one another. Racial tensions were driving a social justice movement that shined a spotlight on injustices that have plagued our nation from its beginnings. Trump and his supporters were spreading the "Big Lie," proclaiming that the 2020 presidential election was "stolen" from him, inciting the January 6th insurrection and desecration of the U.S. Capitol. At critical moments when we need to keep informed and stay safe, there was and still is increasing distrust in news purveyors whom we rely on for timely and accurate information. This is compounded by the unprecedented amount of disinformation fueled by political leaders who attempt to rewrite our history with "alternative facts."

As I finish writing this book, the need for news literacy is more urgent than ever. The partisan divide is deepening as the baseless claims of the "Big Lie" continue to be pushed by Trump and his loyalists, including some conservative news personalities. This is despite that the House Select Committee's televised hearings on the January 6th attack on the Capitol presented overwhelming evidence about the coordinated effort to overturn the 2020 presidential election and Trump's "dereliction of duty" for his inaction during the siege. According to the Justice

Department, more than 1,000 individuals have been arrested, several hundred charged with assaulting, resisting, and impeding police officers or employees, including more than a hundred with using a deadly or dangerous weapon or causing serious bodily injury to an officer, and dozens charged with seditious conspiracy for their role in the insurrection.

It has since been revealed that the "Big Lie" is even bigger than previously known. Email and text evidence shows that Fox News executives, producers and news personalities privately stated that they knew the election fraud allegation was untrue yet publicly perpetuated the lie to appeal to their audience and drive ratings and profits. This information was disclosed in the 1.6 billion dollar defamation lawsuit brought against Fox News by Dominion Voting Systems, the company accused of rigging the vote in the election conspiracy. Court documents also divulged that Rupert Murdoch, chairman of Fox Corporation, admitted under oath that some high-profile network personalities promoted the false election narrative and that he could have stopped them but chose not to intervene. Just before the trial was to begin, Dominion settled for 787.5 million dollars. Fox was held accountable and acknowledged that they made false claims about the 2020 election. Less than a week later, Fox fired Tucker Carlson, at the time the most watched primetime Fox News host and persistent purveyor of the "Big Lie" conspiracy. This case has significant implications for news organizations' responsibility to tell the truth and not misinform the public by promoting disinformation.

Before the Dominion-Fox settlement and Carlson's termination, as the lawsuit against Fox News was unfolding, Republican House Speaker Kevin McCarthy fueled the Fox agenda by giving Tucker Carlson exclusive access to 41,000 hours of the January 6th Capitol surveillance footage to shape his ideologically-based storyline downplaying the attack and its impact on democracy. Carlson's version edited out hours of violent combat between police and the attackers and claimed that his evidence showed the attack was mostly peaceful and not deadly, and most of the attackers were "sightseers" and not insurrectionists. Other news outlets demanded the tapes be made publicly available to ensure the historical record reflects the truth.

Misinformation and disinformation are impacting the health of our nation. As the government officially ends the Covid-19 emergency phase, false and inaccurate information continues to impede the ability of public health professionals to minimize infections and treat serious health complications. Covid and its variants have taken more than one million American lives and show no sign of going away. Living with Covid is the new normal, yet mask mandates and other protective measures have been relaxed, and anti-maskers, anti-vaxxers, and conspiracy theorists are as vocal as ever. False and misleading information is spreading about abortion since the Supreme Court overturned Roe v. Wade, the 50-year precedent guaranteeing abortion rights to women, and many states are outlawing and criminalizing abortion. After decades of pseudoscience and climate deniers undermining climate policy, the severity of the crisis has led many countries to declare a climate emergency for humanity, however, political divisions prevent the United States from invoking an emergency, and instead plans are to expand existing climate programs.

Mass shootings that are motivated by conspiracy theories and hateful ideologies, or that generate them afterward for political or economic gain, are on the rise. The role that these conspiracy theories play in victimizing our country is having its day in court. The Sandy Hook Elementary School massacre in Newtown, Connecticut, which took the lives of 20 children and six adults, has been a target of right-wing radio host Alex Jones who claimed that the murders were staged and the parents and children were actors. After more than a decade of calling Sandy Hook a hoax, Jones and his company Infowars were found guilty of spreading a conspiracy theory and ordered to pay more than one billion dollars to the victims' families. In Buffalo, New York, an 18-year-old White male methodically murdered 10 Black people shopping at a local supermarket, while apologizing to White shoppers and livestreaming the attack on Twitch from a helmet-mounted camera. He said he was motivated by the "great replacement" conspiracy theory, which asserts that Whites are being replaced by ethnic and minority groups. The teenage gunman was indicted on domestic terrorism charges motivated by hate and sentenced to life in prison without parole.

Perhaps one of the most horrific 21st century disinformation campaigns to which the world is bearing witness is the unprovoked and unlawful invasion of Ukraine ordered by Russian dictator Vladimir Putin. He has imposed unparalleled press censorship to spread propaganda, hiding the truth from Russians that their country has caused reckless devastation, death and displacement of millions of Ukrainians. Russian activists who speak out against the war are arrested and journalists who write critical coverage about their country's military operations are serving up to 15 years in prison for publishing "fake news." After one year of war with no end in sight, President Volodymyr Zelensky and the Ukrainian people continue to stand their ground, while conspiracy theories on social media attempt to undermine their fight for freedom, and Putin and the Russian military have been accused of committing war crimes.

In the future, natural-language artificial intelligence capable of auto-generating content will make it easier to find information but more challenging to separate fact from fiction. This generation of AI chatbots can have a conversation with a person and respond with text and images that it gathers from the Internet. News organizations are experimenting with these tools to assist in information-gathering as well as to produce certain types of content. Chatbots can generate a plausible news story and conjure up a realistic image, even create a bogus news site and fabricate a news reporter, but they cannot cover breaking news, scoop a story or get an exclusive interview, sense if a source is not telling the truth, or fact-check at the level of quality journalism. The story might contain factual errors, biased information or made-up quotes, plagiarize sources or violate copyright, or spew false narratives and conspiracy theories, intentionally or unintentionally, that can undermine trust in the news. As the technology improves and these types of errors are minimized, news organizations will have to decide how generative AI tools fit journalism's code of ethics and its truth-telling mission, which require verification, independence, accountability, and transparency. Regardless of the AI policies journalists decide, others will be using chatbots to generate different types of content that will exist alongside quality journalism in the media ecosystem, and the burden will fall even more on news consumers to determine who wrote the story and fact-check its accuracy.

News media literacy is an essential life skill. We need to know how to find reliable and credible information from trustworthy sources. We need to understand the news process and how to fact-check the evidence and detect bias. We need to be aware of journalism practices and standards and why the First Amendment and a free press matter. We need to be mindful of how we navigate the information universe and what we consume, create and share online. Each of us has a responsibility to act as a watchdog of truth to prevent misinformation and disinformation from undermining democracy. Facts matter because truth matters in a democracy.

A Few Resources

When we go online, we come across a lot of different types of information. What should we look for to spot false and misleading information? Here is a list of the main types of misinformation and disinformation that we might encounter in the digital media ecosystem and selected groups and organizations that offer news and media literacy resources.

Types of Misinformation and Disinformation

Clickbait: attention-grabbing, exaggerated or sensationalized headlines or photos designed to distract, increase page views and drive ad revenue by enticing the reader to click the link, which typically leads to content that does not match what the reader anticipated based on the text or visuals.

Conspiracy theory: an explanation for an event or circumstance that rejects the widely-accepted official version and instead credits the action to a sinister and/or powerful group. Conspiracy theories usually contain a kernel of truth and cite proof supported by correlational and not causal evidence that often is based on incorrect assumptions. Conspiracies tend to be politically or economically motivated, in-group driven by confirmation bias, usually in response to fear or uncertainty, and attempt to simplify a complex situation.

Deepfake/cheapfake: digitally manipulated video in which an existing image of a person or sound of their voice is replaced with someone else's likeness and/or voice using sophisticated computer-generated techniques. The intent is to deceive by making it appear that a person may have been somewhere they had not actually been or said something that they had not actually said. Initially used to create fake celebrity porn videos, revenge porn and hoaxes, deepfakes are employed to produce fraudulent narratives usually for political purposes. Cheapfakes are more common and popular because they use less expensive and more accessible technology or no software at all to alter the image or voice. For example, cheapfakes can be created by editing an image with Photoshop to change a person's appearance or slowing down the speed of a video to make it sound like a person is slurring their words.

Doctored content: editing original text, photos, or other content to create a false context that supports a fake story or disinformation campaign. Differs from deepfakes and cheapfakes because the intent may not be to pass for real information.

Doxxing (or doxing): online threat to privacy by publicly disclosing personal or identifying information that was meant to be private — such as home address, email, phone number, workplace, sexuality — typically with malicious intent to embarrass, bully, harass or get revenge and cause emotional distress or physical harm to an individual, group, business or organization. Information may be known to the perpetrator or obtained by searching publicly available databases and social media sites or hacking into an account.

Error: a mistake made by a journalist or news organization that is not intended to harm and will be publicly corrected and, if appropriate, issued an apology. Although journalists correct these reporting mistakes, disinformation creators often widely share the uncorrected version or use it as part of their messaging.

Fabricated content: content that is entirely false created to make people think it is real and is usually intended for harmful purposes. Fabricated content is sometimes used to disseminate a specific message for a short period of time, such as a political campaign, and often uses bots for malicious intent.

False context/attribution: real image, headline, quote, caption or other content that is falsely attributed to an event or person to change its meaning.

Gaslighting: a form of psychological manipulation used to make people question their own reality, perceptions, judgment or memory by persistently lying, withholding, denying, contradicting or misdirecting information in an attempt to destabilize a person or group and delegitimize their beliefs. Gaslighting involves a power dynamic in which the victims are fearful of challenging the false narrative.

Hoax: a fake news story, meme, phishing email, clickbait or other Internet item that intentionally pretends to be real to trick someone into believing something is true when it is actually false. People are taken in because hoaxes often play on their confirmation bias about a belief. Hoaxes can be humorous and have a benign impact such as an April Fool's Day prank or a malicious intent such as luring a person to click on a virus-infected link, stealing private information from their device, or worse, swatting a person usually for revenge. Swatting is enabled by doxxing and involves falsely reporting a dangerous situation to provoke a law enforcement or emergency team response against the victim, intentionally putting that person in harms' way.

Imposter content: content created to impersonate genuine websites, social media profiles, brand logos or other media form with the intent to deceive people into believing it is authentic.

Knowledge hole: the purposeful exclusion or simplification of a topic or event to make truth better fit a specific narrative. This includes the erasure or revision of historical events or representing events with too narrow or too broad a focus. Sometimes knowledge holes rely on misinformation that ignores changes in laws or policy, new scientific findings or current events.

Propaganda: news, advertising, entertainment or other information designed to purposefully manipulate what people think and do by using deception to override facts and appeal to emotions. Propaganda is primarily intended to influence political views and actions, such as voting, in negative or positive ways to build mass support and gain power. Techniques include reducing complex issues to catchy slogans and attention-getting images that can easily be remembered, appealing to emotions that play on fears, weaknesses or desires, exaggerating promises and outcomes of success without evidence to support them, and framing messages to exacerbate divisions between people, groups and ideologies.

Pseudoscience: statements, beliefs, theories or practices that claim to be based on factual evidence and grounded in the scientific method but are neither supported by facts nor science and pose potential harm to individuals and society. People who believe or promote pseudoscience might misinterpret the facts, misunderstand the scientific process, rely on outdated or disproven claims, favor confirmation bias over facts, or do so for political or economic reasons. Popular examples are climate change deniers, anti-vaccine advocates, and miracle cure enthusiasts.

Satire/parody: the use of humor, exaggeration or irony to expose, critique or ridicule the ignorance, flaws or shortcomings of a person, organization, policy, or society itself. Articles, memes, skits, songs, and other formats that use satire or parody are usually intended as constructive social commentary about contemporary politics and newsworthy issues. Although the intent is not to deceive, people who do not understand the comedic nature can mistakenly believe that the information is true. Satire is also used to bypass fact-checking, spread rumors or conspiracies, and dismiss misleading claims or disinformation by politicians.

Sponsored content: a type of native advertising made to look like a legitimate video, news article, opinion piece or other editorial content to help advertisers reach their audience. Sponsored content is deceptive because it is designed to fit the format and user experience where it appears and is not clearly labeled to let consumers know it is a paid advertisement.

Selected News and Media Literacy Resources

Center for Media Literacy

https://www.medialit.org

The Center for Media Literacy (CML) is a pioneer in the field of media literacy providing leadership, professional development, and evidence-based educational resources and tools to teach media literacy skills and strategies. Its media literacy framework of key questions and core concepts is used by educators around the world to help prepare students for living and learning in a global media culture.

Center for News Literacy at Stony Brook

https://www.centerfornewsliteracy.org/

The Center for News Literacy is a university program that teaches students how to use critical thinking skills to judge the reliability and credibility of news. Its Digital Resource Center serves as a clearinghouse for news literacy curricula and resources for educators, students, and the public.

Common Sense Media

https://www.commonsensemedia.org/

Common Sense Media is a leading source of entertainment and technology recommendations for families, conducts original research about media and children, and offers digital citizenship and media and news literacy resources and lessons for K-12.

Crash Course

https://www.youtube.com/c/crashcourse

Crash Course is an educational YouTube channel that offers courses on a range of topics. They partnered with MediaWise, Poynter Institute, and Stanford History Education Group to develop "Navigating Digital Information," a 10-part series of hands-on skills to help evaluate the information we read online.

Duke University Reporters' Lab

https://reporterslab.org/fact-checking/

Duke Reporters' Lab tracks the latest fact-checking news and maintains a database of fact-checking websites around the world that features an interactive map to locate sites in North America, South America, Europe, Asia, Africa and Australia.

Information Futures Lab

https://sites.brown.edu/informationfutures/

Information Futures Lab at Brown University brings together a multidisciplinary network of researchers and practitioners to collaborate on problem-solving the obstacles that prevent effective communication. Their goal is to design and implement solutions that help communities build trust, mitigate misinformation, and protect the future of our information ecosystem.

Media Education Lab

https://mediaeducationlab.com/

The Media Education Lab at the University of Rhode Island networks educators to advance research and scholarship in media and digital literacy and provides multimedia curriculum resources and professional development programs, including webinars, online learning communities, a Summer Institute, and a Graduate Certificate Program in Digital Literacy.

National Association for Media Literacy Education

https://namle.net/

The National Association for Media Literacy Education (NAMLE) is the largest nonprofit membership organization dedicated to advancing media literacy education in the United States. As the leading media literacy voice in the U.S., NAMLE hosts the annual National Media Literacy Week and provides leadership, advocacy, networking and resources with the goal "to make media literacy highly valued and widely practiced as an essential life skill."

News Literacy Project

https://newslit.org/

The News Literacy Project is a nonpartisan education nonprofit that provides programs and resources for teachers, students and the public to help them become engaged and informed news-literate citizens. Its Checkology virtual platform is a free resource with lessons to learn to identify credible information, seek out reliable sources, and apply critical thinking skills to separate fact-based content from falsehoods.

NewseumED/Freedom Forum

https://newseumed.org/

NewseumED is the education arm of the Freedom Forum, a nonpartisan public policy center whose mission is to foster First Amendment freedoms for all. NewseumED offers free resources to increase public understanding of the importance of the First Amendment and a free press and cultivate media literacy skills essential to civic life through student classes, educator trainings, and other learning tools. In addition, Freedom Forum provides access to Today's Front Pages of newspapers around the country and conducts an annual survey of Americans' views and knowledge about the First Amendment.

NiemanLab

https://www.niemanlab.org/

The Nieman Journalism Lab focuses on the future of quality journalism as the Internet and digital technology transform the news business. The Lab encourages a collaborative exchange of ideas and invites journalists to join the conversation to help figure out the changing role of journalism. It is an initiative of the Nieman Foundation for Journalism at Harvard whose mission is to promote and elevate the standards of journalism.

Poynter Institute

https://www.poynter.org

The Poynter Institute is "the world's leading instructor, innovator, convener and resource for anyone who aspires to engage and inform citizens." Its *MediaWise* program empowers people of all ages to become critical consumers of online content. The *Teen Fact-Checking Network* is a virtual newsroom of teens who use social media storytelling to show step-by-step how to debunk viral misinformation and disinformation. *On Campus* trains campus correspondents to facilitate fact-checking sessions online and in college classrooms across the country. The teen virtual newsroom is a verified signatory of Poynter's *International Fact-Checking Network's Code of Principles,* which promotes a global exchange of fact-checking best practices to advance accountability in journalism.

Project Look Sharp

https://projectlooksharp.org

Project Look Sharp is a nonprofit outreach program at Ithaca College that offers media literacy curriculum resources and professional development to help K-16 educators enhance students' critical thinking and civic engagement.

RAND Corporation

https://www.rand.org/research/projects/truth-decay.html

RAND Corporation's multi-faceted Truth Decay initiative examines "the diminishing role of facts and analysis in public life" and ways to counter it. Its researchers identified media literacy education as a powerful tool to engage young people in civic life and counteract disinformation by changing how they consume, create, and share information.

Stanford History Education Group

https://cor.stanford.edu/

The Stanford History Education Group (SHEG) is an award-winning research and development team that creates free evidence-based lessons and assessments to develop critical thinking and analysis of historical events and online information. Its Civic Online Reasoning (COR) curriculum is at the cutting-edge of developing the essential skills students need to navigate the digital landscape and evaluate online content.